MW01121457

The Virtual Assistant's Guide To Marketing

The VA Approach to Marketing Your Services

The Virtual Assistant's Guide

To Marketing

The VA Approach to Marketing Your Services

Michelle Jamison

ISBN: 1-932205-67-5
Library of Congress Control Number: 2003096145

Word Association Publishers
205 5th Avenue
Tarentum, PA 15084
www.wordassociation.com

CONTENTS

◆

ACKNOWLEDGEMENTS

I'm extremely proud of this book, not because I am the author or the time I spent feverishly writing, but because it is specifically for Virtual Assistants.

Being a Virtual Assistant is not only my profession – it is my passion. I am passionate about everything it means to be a Virtual Assistant: the professionalism it takes, the independence it creates and, above all else, the feeling of finding my place.

The world of Virtual Assistance is a unique and special place; beyond the technology lies a very heart-centered, supportive group of extraordinary individuals. It is to those VA's that I dedicate this book.

Among this group are some very special individuals who deserve my thanks. To Mary-Lou, who introduced me to the profession and if she hadn't, I would not be writing this today. To my team of fantastic VA's and very special friends, Laura, Carol, Paula, Macrina, thank you for all that you do and allowing me the space to write this. To my dear friend and confidant, Amy who inspired me to be all that I can be and to never look back.

A special thank-you to the two men in my life, my husband Bruce and my son Jacob, who supportively put up with the long hours, late nights and lost time. I love you both!

Lastly...Thank you Mom & Dad.

ABOUT THIS BOOK

This book focuses on the VA approach to marketing. To sum it up: building relationships by providing superior customer service, building trust and confidence and, by doing so, generating word of mouth and referrals. You will read about this approach as well as other traditional marketing initiatives, such as advertising, networking, marketing plans and how to integrate into your virtual practice.

So let's begin...we have a lot to cover!

An Introduction to Marketing

*Your ability to set goals and to make plans for their accomplishment
is the master skill of success.*
-- Brian Tracy

You will find numerous definitions of the term "marketing." Every textbook, workbook or article you read may have a different definition of marketing. One popular definition and one which is fitting when marketing a VA practice is "*Marketing is anything you do to get or keep a customer.*" This definition, from Harvard professor Michael Porter is simple but very true. It is the process of reaching out to new clients and providing superior customer service to keep current clients content with you and your services.

Many people confuse the terms "marketing" and "sales" thinking that marketing is a fancy word for "sales". However, selling your service is not the be all and end all of marketing. A sale is the point at which the service is offered, it is an important part of the marketing process - but it is not a replacement.

The same confusion occurs over the term "advertising." Although advertising is an important part of the marketing process it is just that – only a part. Advertising is the way in which you get the "word out" about your services.

Think of marketing your services as a continuous cycle.

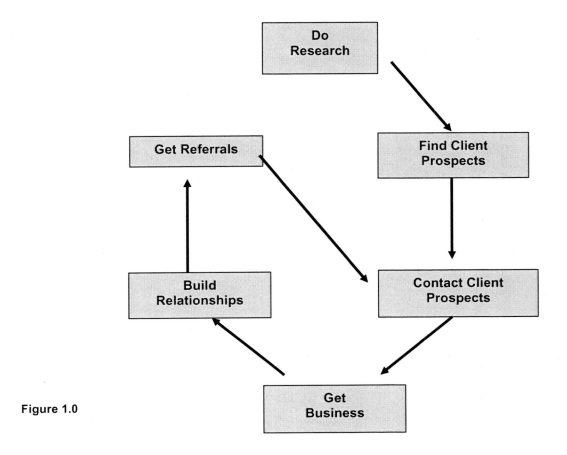

Figure 1.0

As you follow the marketing cycle, you will encounter these steps:

1. The marketing cycle begins with research. Research will help you acquire the knowledge and information to find your prospective clients.
2. When you have found your prospective clients, it is time to get the "word out" about what you are offering and how it will benefit them.
3. If they are impressed with what they are being offered and have a need for that service, it will result in business for you.
4. When you are providing services to your clients, relationships are being built.
5. If you are providing superior customer service to your current clients and they are content, they will feel comfortable giving you referrals and, ultimately, the cycle will repeat with each new client.

The VA Approach to Marketing

The VA approach to marketing is not all about personal selling or advertising. The VA approach to marketing focuses on relationship-based marketing. Relationship-based marketing includes networking, referral-based marketing, niche identification and development, customer service driven, and the continuous value-added approach. Also important are more traditional forms of marketing and promotions (market identification, advertising, public relations and research).

As a Virtual Assistant, you will find that your long-term clients are based more on relationships than about the services you are offering. Ultimately your goal is to provide high-quality services but equally important is to build solid working relationships. In order to build these relationships you must be clear about a few points:

- Who are you
- Who is your ideal client
- What benefits does your service bring to the relationship

Who are you? This may seem like a simple question to answer but is it? What are some of your personal traits that you feel will help you to excel in this field? What is it about who you are, that will make you the ideal Virtual Assistant?

When we are marketing our services, we are in fact marketing ourselves; it is very different than marketing a tangible, unemotional product. Marketing your services is a much more personal transaction and can result in a feeling of rejection when people do not hire you. In order to be attractive to others, and gain their trust, you need to project precisely the person to whom they are entering into a relationship with.

A simple way to help you start the process is to be clear about your uniqueness and how you differ from others in the VA profession. These differences can be personality traits, technical skills, the types of clients you serve or other factors that make up who you are.

Who is your ideal client? There is no better feeling than being hired by a new client, the excitement of someone new to work with, the anticipation of possibilities and the added finances. However, is this new client your ideal client and do you know who your ideal client is?

It is important very early in your VA practice to determine the type of client with whom you deem your "ideal client." Remember we are talking about relationship-based marketing. In order to have an effective client/VA relationship, you have to be just as comfortable with your client as they need to be with you; a mutual respect and admiration needs to be present.

As individuals, we are not likely to marry or be committed to someone who is not our ideal mate, someone who we could not picture spending the rest of our lives with. So why develop a working relationship with someone who instinctively you know is not a match?

How will you know if this person is not a match? At the end of a 15 minute conversation with a prospective client, you will know whether or not that person is someone who you would like to work with. Your "gut instinct" will tell you…listen to it.

In order to clearly define your ideal client, start by writing a list of all the qualities and characteristics you are looking for in a client. These can be personal and/or professional characteristics. For example, your ideal client may be someone who communicates effectively, is internet savvy, pays on time, has a sense of humor, and respects that you have a life outside of work.

Keep in mind that 70% or as high as 90% of a VA's business comes from referrals and word of mouth. Hold true to the picture of your ideal client. Financial gain is never a good reason to start a relationship that is destined to fail and could inevitably come back to haunt you.

What benefits does your service bring to the relationship? Number one question that your prospects will want to know is "What can you do for me?" You need to be clear on the benefits that you bring to this working relationship. How can you assist a prospective client?

Knowing the benefits that your services provide will both attract more clients and help you serve them better.

Features vs. Benefits
An important distinction and one of the more basic principles or marketing is features versus benefits. Features are the aspects of your service whereas **benefits** are what people get from using your service.

Generally most business owners decide to start a business based on two things:

1) What service they can provide that they are good at
2) What they assume customers will buy.

Often these assumptions are correct, however some small business marketers believe that prospects will understand why they should buy the product or use the service just because they have been told about it. Therefore, business owners only communicate the features of their product or service to prospective customers and neglect to mention the benefits.

Examples of Features and Benefits for VA Services:

Feature:	Benefit:
Document Preparation	Clients will look good to their clients with professional looking documents.
Travel Arrangements	Clients do not have to deal with the aggravation of booking a flight.
Reminder Services	Clients look like the hero when they remember their families' or clients' birthdays.
Bookkeeping	They have freedom from fear of maintaining accurate books when the "tax man" comes around.

Features do not entice people to hire you; benefits do. They answer the question "What's in it for me?"

In order to begin marketing your service, it is important that you clearly define what the benefits are in a way that your client can relate.

Marketing on a Budget

There is a big difference in big business versus small business marketing; although the process may be the same, the similarities end there. You are obviously not going to be able to market your VA service the same way as a huge corporation such as Nike.

Here's why:

Dollars...need I say more?
As an owner of a VA practice, you can already guess one big difference between your marketing strategy and those at Nike headquarters. You guessed it. The big guys have the big budgets. When they talk marketing, they talk hundreds of thousands of dollars. As a VA when we talk marketing budget, we are talking a couple hundred dollars.

Staffing...what staff?
Nike has a marketing vice president. As a VA you have...well, just you! Big businesses have a team of marketing experts at their disposal from advertising directors, sales managers, research directors, customer service specialists and more. In a VA practice you are responsible for all aspects of marketing.

Strategy...what's that?
Each employee in a big business is given a copy of the company's business plan the moment they are hired. Small businesses hear the term "business plan" and run in fear.

Although you may envy the dollars, people and strategic determination of big business, small business does have some advantages. A majority of large corporations spend millions of dollars to fund research to get to know and understand their customers. Meanwhile, a small business owner can pick up the phone and simply talk to their clients at no cost.

Because marketing is to build and maintain customer relationships, for this reason alone small business has the edge.

Budgeting your money and time

The most important thing that you can do in terms of marketing is to establish a realistic budget for your practice.

Businesses such as VA practices normally market to other businesses – such as consultants and real estate agents – and tend to allocate a lower percentage of their monthly revenues to marketing.

There is no set amount that is customary for a VA to set aside for marketing, keeping in mind that most of your clients will be coming from referrals and word of mouth. As a VA, you do not need to spend thousands of dollars on a marketing campaign. Be very selective how and to whom you market your services. Who you market your services to will directly affect your marketing budget.

A step to help you figure out your budget is to look at what you expect your business to accomplish over the upcoming year and what level of marketing is necessary to accomplish the task.

Just as important as budgeting money is budgeting time to spend on marketing. You want marketing to become something that you do naturally and comfortably and woven throughout your day. You should start by budgeting a little time on a regular basis for your marketing initiatives. Whether it is researching potential clients, writing a letter, or finding cost-effective advertising, take an hour or two out of your day.

Major Marketing Categories

Let's explore marketing in terms of categories. Figure 1.1 shows the seven major types or categories to marketing.

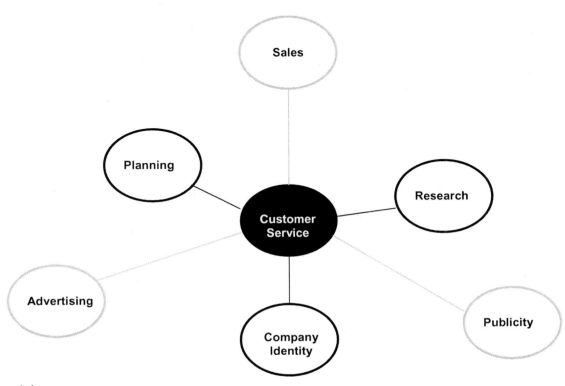

Figure 1.1

Customer Service

The center of Figure 1.1 represents the most important part of marketing a VA practice, customer service. This is what you *do* to *keep* your clients happy and get referrals. Customer service should receive the majority of your marketing attention.

Internal Categories

Research & Planning

Research and Planning is the basis for all your marketing efforts. With research you will gather information about your target market, what advertising works, what does not, what services people need and how much they are willing to pay.

Planning will give you focus on what it is you want to achieve; all of us need some sort of a plan.

Company Identity
People are hiring you and your company, therefore you need to look the part. Your company identity is the various characteristics by which you and your service are recognized and known.

External Categories

Advertising
Advertising is bringing your service to the attention of potential and current clients. Brochures, direct mailings, email messages and even personal contact are all forms of advertising.

Publicity
Publicity is mention in the media. It is a traditional form of exposure that you do not have to pay for and is very effective. If you are mentioned in an article or story, or if you write a column that is published, you will find that it will generate more interest than advertising and cost much less.

Sales
Sales delivers the personal touch; Virtual Assistants usually sell their service primarily by phone or in some cases face-to-face. This gives you a chance to receive client feedback and potentially change how you sell your services by people's reaction.

Identify Your Target Market

In order to effectively market your Virtual Assistant practice, it is important first to identify your target market or, in other words, those individuals who you want to work for…your clients.

Knowing your target market just makes good business sense. It will uncover and help you to identify potential problems and help you recognize opportunities in the marketplace that you could potentially have missed. Identifying your target market will save you energy, time and money by focusing your efforts on those individuals who are more apt to hire your services.

How will your clients find you unless you figure out who will need your service?

It is important that you establish some parameters to help you identify your target market. Begin by asking yourself some questions:

1. Who is your ideal client?
2. What are their needs?
3. What benefits do they want?
4. Where are these clients located?
5. What is their concern about your type of service?
6. Who is your competition?

We have already discussed question 1 and 3 earlier; let's take a look at the rest.

What are their needs?
When a client hires a Virtual Assistant, what is this telling you?

o They need support
o Their business is growing
o They may not have the skills
o They need a professional image
o They do not have the space for on-site assistance

Where are they located?
The wonderful thing about being a Virtual Assistant and working virtually is that your clients can be anywhere. However, this does not really help you much when determining how to target your market. Some Virtual Assistants prefer to do work within their own town, city, even province or state, while others prefer specific countries. In most cases Virtual Assistants choose to work with individuals from all different walks of life. This is one of the perks about this profession; you get to experience so many different cultures.

Some things you may want to consider are:

- Time zones
- Currency difference
- Communication
- Costs associated with distance

What is their concern about your type of service?

One of the best things about being a Virtual Assistant can also be one of the worst in terms of getting clients. You work virtually, which means most of the time your clients may never see you up close and personal. To someone who has not worked in this type of environment, it can be a little challenging. Issues of giving up control and questions of whether you are working when you say you are working are concerns for many newcomers to the virtual environment.

Who is your competition?

Who else out there provides the same or a similar service to you? This could be other VA's, Temporaries, Agencies, etc. This would be a good time for you to do some research on your competitive market. A competitive market is those individuals with whom you share a market, who you are competing with for clients. As a Virtual Assistant your main competitors will be other Virtual Assistants. However, there are other competitors that you will want to research as well. Temporary and employment agencies are starting to realize that most administrative work can be done from home. Research all aspects of your competitive market.

Target Marketing: Rifle vs. Shotgun

When talking about target marketing, it is important that we touch on the concept of rifle versus shotgun.

Rifle marketing: You are clear on whom it is you are aiming your marketing message. You have a particular type of client to whom you are marketing your services.

Shotgun marketing: You are spraying your message all over the place hoping that some of it will hit. You are unclear of the type of client that would use your services so you bombard everyone with your marketing message.

Accuracy is better and more cost-effective.

Developing a Niche

Finding a niche could be one of the most important things you do for your business. As a Virtual Assistant you will find that there are many specific professions that would benefit from hiring a VA.

Developing a niche takes target marketing a step further. If your target market is small business or home-based businesses, you will be working harder and spending a lot of money promoting your business. Think of the rifle versus shotgun methods. Developing a niche will ensure that you are targeting those individuals who CAN and NEED your services. As well by developing your niche, you will be working with those individuals you WANT to work with.

A niche market is a defined group that includes the following characteristics:

1. they have the same specialized interest and needs
2. they have a need for your service
3. they can be easily reached within this group
4. the group is large enough to produce the volume of business you need.

The more narrowly you define your niche market, the easier it is to cater to those individuals.

Niches for Virtual Assistants

As a fairly new profession, more and more Virtual Assistants are finding unique and different niches by working with select professions:

- Real Estate Agents
- Lawyers
- Doctors
- Artists
- Professional Coaches
- Consultants
- Professional Speakers
- Dentists
- Web Designers
- And even other VA's

Finding your own niche

One way to find your niche is to evaluate your existing clientele. If you are finding that the majority of your clients are from a particular profession, you may have already found your niche.

However, if you are a new VA and have not yet developed your clientele, you could base your niche on the following:

- a particular profession you have worked for in the past
- the people who you want to work with
- the type of services that you offer
- how you provide these services
- your problem-solving ability

Is there a particular profession you have worked for in the past?
Some Virtual Assistants have years of administrative experience working for a particular profession. Real Estate is one profession that is common among VA niches. Take a look at the individuals or professions that you have worked for in the past; could you assist that profession virtually?

The people who you want to work with
Is there a particular type of person whom you enjoy working for or would like to work for? Some individuals do not necessarily make their niche a profession but a type of person. For some VA's they prefer more creative types such as artists, writers and actors/actresses. Other VA's prefer more extroverted individuals such as real estate agents, sales representatives and professional speakers.

The type of services you offer
Do you have a service that would attract a certain niche? For instance, real estate agents have many, many contacts that they try to juggle. A VA who is fluent with a number of contact databases and management software could be just what they need.

How you provide these services
By offering services virtually, all VA's have developed this niche. However, a niche could be to offer on-site assistance once a month to locally-based clients.

Your problem solving ability
Do you have an understanding of certain types of problems and make that ability a niche? For example, a Virtual Assistant who works primarily with Associations has the ability and experience to deal with and solve problems that go along with association

management. Another example is a VA who has worked in the Human Resources field, who would be able to support his/her clients with the problem of hiring skilled individuals.

Tips on Finding Your Niche

1. **Brainstorm**
   Look around you: opportunities may be closer than you think.

2. **Know yourself**
   Realistically assess your strengths and weaknesses, both professionally and personally. Consider what you enjoy doing and those individuals who you like working for.

3. **Research**
   Talk to other VA's and find out why they like a particular niche.

4. **Focus**
   Focus on the goals for your company and what you hope to accomplish and how a niche may help with these goals.

5. **Prepare**
   Play the "devil's advocate" and anticipate questions from your prospective niche. How would you handle them?

6. **Educate Others**
   Talk to everyone about your niche and be able to project your ideas. Look for feedback.

7. **Plan Ahead**
   Anticipate challenges. If your preferred niche does not work, do you have a contingency plan?

8. **Evaluate**
   Once decided and implemented, step back and assess your niche. Is it all that you thought it would be?

Customer Service

As a Virtual Assistant, providing great customer service is the most effective and least expensive way of marketing. The majority of your marketing time and budget should be spent on building solid relationships with clients.

You can spend thousands of dollars marketing your service but if you are not good at what you do, your clients will not come back. Worst of all, they will tell others that your services are not up to par. Word of mouth travels fast.

Even if you are a new VA starting your practice, you should still be thinking of the value that you will be bringing your potential clients. As a VA, at least 70% of your business will be and should be from past clients and their referrals.

Some things to think about:

1. It is more expensive to get a new client than to keep an existing client.
2. You work more efficiently with existing clients since you are already familiar with their situations.
3. In order to produce superior customer service you must love what it is you are doing.

Three L's of Superior Customer Service

Listen

> Listen to your clients, make them feel heard. Superior customer service starts with listening to your clients' wants, needs, concerns and ideas. When you are distracted from conversations, clients will feel your disinterest and not feel looked after.

Learn

> Even if you are unsure of something, your clients will appreciate the fact that you are taking the initiative to learn about their problem, their product, their service, or about what is important to them. It makes them feel that you are sincerely interested in what it is that they are doing.

Love

> Most of all love what you are doing. If you are not happy doing your job, it will reflect in your productivity, your personality and, above all else, the quality of your work.

Adding Client Value

Having loyal clients can amount in a lot of business for you over their lifetime. In order to receive that loyalty, you need to add value to the client/VA relationship. Providing value to the client can be as simple as answering the phone in a genuinely, warm and inviting way.

Being the nature in which VA's work is primarily phone and email, it is important to add those personal touches to all aspects of your customer service especially when it relates to the telephone.

Some items to consider are:

Answering the phone
- When answering the phone sound glad that your client is calling you.
- Always be professional, however, clients will appreciate warmth in your voice. Try answering the phone like you know it is a friend.
- Develop an appropriate greeting, for example, "Mary Wilson, how can I help you?"

Returning Calls
- When a client calls you, try to return the call within two hours.
- If your client is unreachable when you call back, try again and leave specific hours when you can be reached.
- Email your client as well and let them know that you received their message and are available to speak with them.

Email
- Be concise and to the point. Your clients will appreciate a short direct email.
- Email them updates on particular projects to keep them "in the loop".
- Check your email at least every 20 minutes in order to return urgent client enquires.
- Don't get too carried away with "emoticons" however a well placed smiley face ☺ periodically may lighten up the day for your client.

Client Extras

Little things really do make a big difference. The smallest gestures made on your part can make your clients feel special and coming back for more. Deliver an "above and beyond the call of duty" service to all your clients. By doing this you will be adding value to the relationship and intensifying that customer loyalty.

What client extras can you give?

- When doing a large project for a client, take off an hour or two on the final bill and indicate that there was no charge. Clients will appreciate the fact that you are attuned to their budget.
- Call or email your client just to say, "Hi, how are you?" This will let them know that you are thinking of them.
- If you are going to be away from your office for even a day, let your clients know this. They will feel taken care of and informed.
- If you come across information that may serve your client, send it to them at no charge.
- For special occasions, send your client an e-card or hard-copy card. A small gift would be a wonderful surprise for them.
- Offer your clients an hour a week free for strategic planning sessions.
- Survey their client service and satisfaction. Ask them what you can do to provide added value.

Chapter One - Summary

By now you should have an understanding of the basics of marketing and the VA approach to marketing. By understanding the general ideas behind marketing in terms of concept, approach, categories, target markets and budgeting you have developed a framework which will help you develop a niche. Develop a niche in which people appreciate what you do, the services you provide and the way in which you deliver those services so you are able to enjoy what you are doing, make money and above all else provide superior customer service.

This is what marketing is all about!

Company Identity

*Decide upon your major definite purpose in life
and then organize all your activities around it.*
-Brian Tracy

Creating a company identity is an important part of every business; your company identity presents an image of how the rest of the world, including potential clients, will recognize you and your services.

This chapter will examine the importance of your company's identity and explain how you can create and project an image that will help you sell your services.

Company Identity vs. Company Image

Although very similar in meaning, company identity and company image are two different things. Your company identity can be defined as the various characteristics by which you and your service are recognized and known. Therefore, your company image is how your business identity is perceived by customers, associated professionals, the media, and the public at large.

McDonalds, for example, is known for pioneering the fast food industry. Most consumers are familiar with the "golden arches." The production of hamburgers and soft drinks is one aspect of their identity. But how is McDonalds perceived? What image does it project?

There are many characteristics that go into creating your company identity: your service, logo, tag line, Vision, Mission, Core Value statements, advertisements, and website are obvious features that tell your potential customers who you are.

You may be thinking "If my service is good, that's all that counts." Not so, while it is essential to have a quality service, the reality is that in today's business world, image sells. You want to project yourself and your company as being reliable, professional and dependable.

For example: You have determined that your target audience is corporate HR consultants. You want to project an image that is professional, straight-laced and confident. Your website should not be plastered with little pink butterfly images and rainbows, the corporate world is not interested in how "pretty" your site looks. They want to see a very professional, direct and well written website that appeals to them.

Creating Your Identity

There are three stages in creating your company's identity:

1) determine your company identity
2) design your company identity
3) communicate your company identity

Determine your Company Identity

Start by asking yourself, "what do I want my customers to say and think about my service and company?" Answering this question will help you determine what kind of identity you want to establish.

When determining your identity, you must understand three important factors:

a. **Type of Business and Service**
If you are reading this book, you have already established that your business is that of a Virtual Assistant. The services you provide will be administrative services. Your image must make sense and match what you do.

b. **Target Market**
When developing your identity, a rule of thumb to follow is that your identity should match the identity of your clients and potential clients.

c. **Your Competitors**
You must also determine the image of your competitors. There are two thoughts on this issue: Some say your own business identity should come close to your competitors and others say that you should stand out from your competition. For the greatest impact, you will want an appropriate blend of the two. You will want to project the image of being reliable and dependable like your competition but you will need an image that gives you a competitive advantage, for example, being new and innovative.

Design your Company Identity

In order to communicate the identity that is right for your business and your target market, you must design it. You will want to establish a consistent look and feel to all your materials. A good place to start is to create your Vision, Mission and Core Values for your company.

These three elements will be the driving force of your business. Vision, Mission and Core Value statements will let everyone know what your business is striving to achieve and the values it instills. Good statements take time and effort – do not rush it.

Vision Statement

According to the Cambridge International Dictionary of English: *"vision: noun [U] the ability to imagine how a country, society, industry, etc. will develop in the future and to plan in a suitable way."*

In simpler terms, a Vision Statement can paint a picture that creates a sense of desire and builds commitment to reaching the vision. It is what you see possible. Your vision statement is about the impact you want to have on the world.

When creating your vision statement, keep it simple, meaningful, and inspiring. It will provide direction and guidance as your business grows.

Your vision statement:

- must meet your company's goals as well as community goals
- is a statement of your values
- is a public declaration of your expected outcomes
- will guide your actions
- will be a key component of strategic planning.

Exercise: Creating Your Vision

Envision it is five years from today's date and you have a successful Virtual Assistant practice.

Respond to the following questions:

1. How has the job market changed?
2. What have I done to prepare for success in this world?
3. What have I been spending most of my time doing?

Benefits of Visualizing

Visualizing:

- Breaks you outside of boundary thinking
- Identifies direction and purpose
- Promotes interest and commitment
- Encourages openness to unique creative solution
- Encourages and builds confidence
- Results in efficiency and productivity

Samples of vision statements for some well-known companies:

Sears

Sears Canada is a full-line, full-service department store and catalogue retailer dedicated to providing its customers with quality merchandise and exceptional service, coast to coast.

Royal Canadian Mounted Police

The RCMP is Canada's national police service. Proud of our traditions and confident in meeting future challenges, we commit to preserve the peace, uphold the law and provide quality service in partnership with our communities.

Astrazeneca Canada Inc. (a pharmaceutical company)

By forging new standards in therapy and establishing new industry benchmarks that improve the health of Canadians, AstraZeneca Canada Inc. will be the pre-eminent pharma company.

Mission Statement

According to the Cambridge International Dictionary of English: *"mission statement: noun [U] A mission statement is a short written description of the aims of a business, charity, government department or public organization."*

The mission statement provides the action for your vision. It will describe what you do to meet your vision.

Your mission statement:

- draws on your vision statement
- must be future oriented and portray your organization as it will be, as if it already exists
- should be focused on one common purpose
- must be a short statement, not more than one or two sentences
- should be easy enough to recite by memory.

Examples of Mission Statements:

Wal-Mart (1990)

Become a $125 billion company by the year 2000

Sony (1950's)
>Become the company most known for changing the worldwide poor-quality image of Japanese products

Boeing (1950)
>Become the dominant player in commercial aircraft and bring the world into the jet age

Ford Motor Company (Early 1900's)
>Ford will democratize the automobile.

Core Values

Many organizations choose to list their core values alongside their vision and mission statements. The core values outline the ethics and values of the organization, creating a pledge to its staff, clients and the world at large. These simple statements demonstrate a company's commitment to success.

Examples of Core Values:

Sears
- Customer-focus
- Results-oriented
- Partnerships/Teamwork
- Pro-active and innovative
- Risk-taking
- Open, honest communications
- Accountability
- Respect
- Diversity

New York Times
- Content of the highest quality and integrity. This is the basis for our reputation and the means by which we fulfill the public trust and our customers' expectations.
- Fair treatment of employees based on respect, accountability and standards.
- Creating long-term shareholder value through investment and constancy of purpose.
- Good corporate citizenship.

Royal Canadian Mounted Police

Recognizing the dedication of all employees, we will create and maintain an environment of individual safety, well-being and development. We are guided by:

Accountability:
There are two components of accountability. The first is the process of rendering an account to those from whom we derive our authority of what we did, why we did it, how we did it and what we are doing to improve performance or results. An important element of this component is accepting the personal consequences of our actions. The second component of accountability is one of answerability - the obligation to provide information to others in our communities of interest with respect to our decisions, actions and results in light of clear, previously agreed upon understandings and expectations. For example, we inform our communities about our actions, but we must render account of our actions to our direct supervisors. In this organization, authorities can be delegated, but accountability cannot.

Respect:
Is the objective, unbiased consideration and regard for the rights, values, beliefs and property of all people.

Professionalism:
Is having a conscientious awareness of our role, image, skills and knowledge in our commitment to quality client oriented service.

Honesty: Is being truthful in character and behaviour.

Compassion: Is demonstrating care and sensitivity in word and action.

Integrity: Is acting consistently with our other core values.

Company Name

Choosing a company name is one of the most exciting parts of starting a business. It adds a sense of reality to the process. A clever business name can be an effective marketing tool, however, coming up with one can also be frustrating. Do not let the search for a perfect business name deter you from starting your business.

Usually the best name for your company is your own after all YOU are the brand. Adding a descriptive phrase to clarify what you do is also suggested.

A good business name accomplishes a number of goals:

- **It is direct.** You do not want anything in your business name that could potentially confuse a potential client about what it is you do.

- **It is not trendy.** Stay away from names that are too closely identified to current trends. Trends come and go.

- **It conveys the right feeling.** You want to choose a name that triggers a positive association.

- **It is easy to spell & pronounce.** Make it simple; a name which is easily spelled is easily remembered. People have a hard time remembering names they cannot pronounce.

- **It is memorable.** It is hard enough choosing a name not to mention one that is memorable. Of course this is not always possible.

- **It is pleasing to the ear.** Whether something is pleasing or not has a lot to do with your market.

Once you have a list of prospective names, share these with family, friends and colleagues.

OOPS!!

Larger companies spend thousands of dollars researching potential names for products and services and sometimes they even fail.

General Motors introduced the Chevy Nova into Latin America and it was a total disaster. You see, in Spanish, "No va" means "doesn't go".

Company Logo

When establishing your identity, there is nothing more critical than your logo. A logo is an image that is associated with your company and gives the public another way to remember you. Your logo appears on all of your correspondence, your business card, letterhead, flyers and advertisements. The purpose of a logo is to convey the essence of your company's identity.

Some individuals are auditory, some are visual; a visual image makes your company more memorable. People use more of their brains when they associate you with both words and image.

The word "logo" means a name, symbols or trademark designed for easy recognition. Logos date back to Greece in ancient times. Many early Greek and Roman coins bear the monograms or logos of rulers or towns. These ciphers consisted of a single letter, and later a design or mark consisting of two or more letters entwined.

In the thirteenth century, logo design evolved from simple ciphers to trademarks for traders and merchants. These early examples of logo design include mason marks, goldsmith marks and watermarks of nobility.

With the emergence of the information age, logo and logo design changed. Today the general public has become increasingly aware of visual symbols, especially trademarks. Logos have now become the front line of a company.

A good logo will convey something about your company, even a feeling. The Nike swoosh represents speed and movement. A logo does not have to be a drawing or illustration. Think of Coca Cola – the words themselves are an illustration. This is called a "logotype," and can be very effective.

When thinking of your logo design, consider these items:

- Make an effort to notice other company logos, especially within the VA profession.
- Graphics: Try to avoid using a lot of graphics. The simpler your design, the more impact it will have. Remember that the purpose of your logo is to quickly make a statement about your company.
- Typestyle: Bold blocks of text invoke the image that the company is strong and large. Italic type can convey a classic image. Whatever typestyle you choose, it needs to be easy to read.
- Tagline: The short and snappy sentence or words that appear underneath a logo is a tagline.

Logo Colour

The colour of your logo is an important element. Bright colours will be strong attention getters and excite people; blues and grays have a conservative theme. To convey the image that you are hot and innovative, use red, yellow and orange.

Here are some common colour & shape associations:

> Blue – reliable, intelligent, secure, business-like, leadership, depressing
> Pink – feminine, calm, relaxing, therapeutic
> Black – rich, sensuous
> White – pure, clean
> Red – danger, bargain, excitement, warm, intimate
> Yellow – sun, outdoors
> Brown – rich, earthy
> Green – money, leisure
> Orange – healthful, warm
> Gray – security

 Feminine, soft, weak, tender, loving, warm

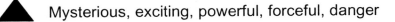 Mysterious, exciting, powerful, forceful, danger

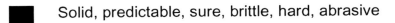 Solid, predictable, sure, brittle, hard, abrasive

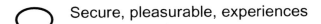 Secure, pleasurable, experiences

A great example of a company that is consistent with colour is American Express. They use the same shade of the colour green throughout all of their marketing materials involving their credit card. The colour green is significant and an inseparable aspect of their logo.

Tip: If budget allows, we highly recommend that you hire a designer to create your logo. A designer will understand the differences between print and web use and will provide you with both. You want to maintain a professional company identity and a well designed logo will help you achieve this.

Tagline

One of the key pieces of your company's identity is your tagline. A tagline is used to better explain what your business does and to create an impression about your company and/or service.

A tagline is one of the most important ways to market your business; it can become the basis of your advertising and marketing pieces. Tag lines do not have to be "catchy" but they should be memorable to your target audience. A general rule is the shorter the better. Most taglines are just a few words. It is not just how short you make it; it is about *how* you make it short.

Here's an easy method to help you create your tagline.

1. Try to express what your business does in one sentence or less. Trim it right down. This is not a mission statement; it is a plain statement of what you do.
    For example: If you provide administrative support to real estate agents, your sentence would be: Providing Administrative Support to Real Estate Agents.

2. List some of the benefits of your service.

3. Put the information from step one and two together and develop several taglines. Remember, your taglines should carry some feeling or emotion as well as convey the benefits of your service.

4. Try these out on your friends or family and pick the best tagline. Pick the one which most aligns with how you see your business.

Use your tagline on all of your materials in conjunction with your logo.

Some well known taglines are:

> Epson: "The power to create"
> De Beer's: "Diamonds are forever"
> Timex: "It takes a licking and keeps on ticking."
> Nike: "Just do it!"

Branding

A book about marketing would not be complete without a few words about branding. Branding is a name, term, design, symbol, feature or identity which distinguishes your service or services from others. Strong brands can deliver incredible customer loyalty and your service could become synonymous with price, quality or some other feature.

Branding is a concept that has received a lot of attention. Many firms have created brands that are well known, from Coca Cola to BMW. BMW is a premium brand of car which conveys the image of prestige and quality, however BMW would not be perceived like this if they did not continue to build high quality cars for which people are willing to pay more than other car "brands".

Do you need to have a "brand"? Not necessarily, some individuals feel that branding is just a new word to give consultants something new to sell and that it is very similar to positioning. If branding appeals to you, use it, but make sure it is consistent with who you are and that it helps you build those very important client and prospective client relationships.

Understanding branding – things you should know:

1. Your brand needs to be always represented.
   Every time a client or prospective client has contact with you, your brand should support a positive image.

2. Branding is a long-term commitment.
   In order for a brand to be effective, it must be in the minds of your clients for a very long time. Consider this when establishing your brand.

3. You can brand anything.
   Anything and everything you offer can be branded.

4. Knowing yourself is important.
   Understanding yourself and your company is important when determining your brand. What are the advantages and disadvantages associated with your brand? To help you with this, ask current clients, friends and family.

5. Your brand is always a work in progress.
   You will never be able to perfect your brand as your clients' needs and emotional responses will change – just grow with them.

6. Be consistent with your design and message.
   Everything from your company should have the same look, feel and message.

7. Your brand should be appropriate to your clients.

Communicate Your Company Identity

Once you have designed your company identity, items such as your business name, logo, and tagline must be integrated into all of your communication materials. Letterhead, envelopes, business cards, and eventually your website, should contain the image that you have established. All of these items and more will become part of your "marketing kit" which will be discussed in subsequent chapters.

Consistency and repetition is key in planting your company image into the minds of your target market.

Chapter 2 - Summary

Creating your company identity is a critical step in the development of any business, especially a virtual business. You want your company identity to tell clients and prospective clients who you are, what you offer, what you value and most of all, to project an identity that attracts those clients that are best suited for your business.

Even though creating your company identity can be somewhat challenging at times, it can also serve as an outlet for your creativity and help you become clearer on what it is you want your business to be. Have fun and put as much of yourself into your business, after all you are selling your services, so in essence you are selling YOU.

Your Marketing Kit
Things to know before you begin.

Start from wherever you are and with whatever you've got.
-Jim Rohn

In Chapters One and Two, we addressed items such as target market, company identity and communicating your identity. Now it is time we put it all together. The next few chapters will be devoted solely to the development of your Marketing Kit *(Marketing Kit is a term we will be using throughout this book to describe your marketing materials as a whole.)* However, before you can create your marketing kit, there are a few things you should know before you begin.

Step 1: You will need to understand a little more about what goes in a marketing kit.

Step 2: You will need to know how to write your message, in a way that sells.

Contents of a Virtual Assistant Marketing Kit

Business Cards
Business cards are a necessity for any marketing kit. You must ensure that you have professional, high-quality business cards that shout PROFESSIONALISM. It is important that your company name and logo be included on your business card to create a streamlined company identity. We highly recommend that you have your cards professionally printed – a networking must!

Letterhead
Your logo should be incorporated on your letterhead in all correspondence again to create a streamlined look to your company and stay true to your company identity. The more your logo gets out there, the more it will be recognized.

Brochure
Brochures are an effective way to get the message out about your business. Brochures offer you the opportunity to list your services, benefits, and other information important to your target. Brochures are great for direct mailings.

Flyer
A flyer is a very cost-effective solution to marketing your services. A flyer is simply a one page summary of who you are, what you do, and what you are offering. Similar to the brochure, you can create this yourself. It is perfect for direct mailing or postings.

Advertisement
One great way of marketing your practice is by advertising. However, this does come at a price: advertising is not cheap. If you have the creative ability to create your own ad, you are one step ahead of the game.

Sales Letter
Sales letters are a way to communicate with prospective clients in a personal way, at their convenience. Whether by direct mail or email, this is a cost-effective way to introduce yourself and your services.

Press release
Not every marketing kit includes a press release and it is not essential to include one. We have included this only as a suggestion.

Monthly newsletter
Whether you create an email newsletter or a hardcopy version with tips and interesting articles, this is really a great marketing piece for you and your business. By creating a newsletter, you are creating value for those who subscribe, not to mention getting your name out there.

Client Information Package
A client information package is a vital marketing piece for a Virtual Assistant practice. This package incorporates all the information a client will need to make the decision to hire you.

It is entirely up to you what you want to include in your Company Marketing Kit: it is dependent on budget, time and skill. In subsequent chapters, we will look at each piece in greater detail and show you how to create the most effective marketing kit for your VA practice.

A Website

This formidable marketing tool allows you to offer your services to clients world-wide. The majority of individuals who work virtually have a website: this is considered to be the best company brochure and one of the best marketing solutions for any business.

With a website, you can incorporate information about you, your company and your services, and communicate your company identity. It is imperative that you hire a professional and experienced web designer, unless of course you have the skills to design it yourself. Keep in mind though, you want your website to represent you in the best possible light: *there is nothing worse than a website that does not function properly and has no aesthetic value.*

Writing Content That Sells

An important starting point when determining what to include in your marketing kit is to decide what you want to communicate. In earlier chapters we discussed things such as who you are and your niche. Now it is time to finalize this in written format. In order to create effective marketing material you need to be clear yourself before you can communicate this to prospects.

Write down the answers to the following questions and make sure you have them in front of you before you try to write any of your marketing materials. This will be a constant reminder of who you are, who your clients are and the message you are trying to project.

1. Who is your target audience? (prospective clients)
2. What do you stand for? (good time to look at your mission statement)
3. What is your company identity?
4. What is different about you?
5. Why should people use your services? (list benefits)

When writing your content, tell your audience in the very first sentence why they should read any further. Get to the point of how they will benefit from what you have to say.

Exercise: Fill in the blanks

I am _____ because I am/do/provide _____

My written material needs to project the image of_____
(company identity) to convince_____ (target audience) that my
services such as_____ would provide_____
(benefits) because _____ (why?)

These statements not only provide you with the basis of your marketing content, they can also be further developed into your 30-second elevator speech which we will address in a later chapter.

Guideline for Effective Writing

Show your personality. Remember when someone is hiring your services they are hiring you. Make sure that your personality is reflected in all the material that you write. Prospective clients will get a feel for the type of individual you are through the words that you write. If you have a healthy sense of humor show this, if you are a caring, considerate person – do not hide it, flaunt it. By putting as much of yourself into your marketing materials, you will attract those clients who relate well to your material, and could potentially be your ideal client. Use your unique personality traits to win clients.

Only write when you feel like it. Writing is an evolutionary process and cannot be forced. The words flow easier when you are in that creative mood. Do not write for the sake of writing, as you will find it will end up in frustration and dissatisfaction of the final outcome. Write when you have something to say.

Where you write is as important as what you write. Some people write better tucked away in seclusion with nothing but a pen and paper. Others enjoy all that technology has to offer, a personal computer with the latest word processing software. Wherever the place, make sure that it is the one place that you are free of interruptions, comfortable and that will allow those creative juices to flow.

Write the words as if you were speaking them. It is amazing how bold you can get when you are writing words. Some people have a tendency to exaggerate about their business, services and skills when it is down on paper. That face-to-face connection is not valid with written materials. When writing your marketing material, make sure that you are as comfortable speaking the words as you are writing them.

Think of your audience. When writing, keep your audience in your mind at all times. Your readers are busy people so do not overcrowd your materials with unnecessary fluff. Be direct with your intentions and offerings. Get right to the meat of your material – what it is that you can do for them. Remember busy people have better things to do than decipher your material.

Bigger is not better. Use short words, short sentences and short paragraphs. You do not need to use big complicated words to get your point across. Using large words does not make you look any smarter; it just makes the reader with the average I.Q. become irritable. Break up your paragraphs to be short and manageable; paragraphs that seem to go on and on with no breaks will make the reader lose interest quickly.

Mistakes look bad. Your material should be error free when it goes to prospective clients. One spelling error can cost you a potential client. VA's are in the business of professional document preparation; if it has a typo, what is that telling the reader? Make sure that all your material is edited and proofed not only by you but also by someone else. Two sets of eyes are better than one and could result in a new client.

Make Your Business Sound Irresistible

Writing your marketing content can seem overwhelming; you want to start out by introducing yourself and your offerings. However, when writing your marketing text it is not just who you are and what you do that will grab the reader's attention, it is *how* you sound to the reader.

By using key descriptive words and phrases, you can make your business sound irresistible to the reader. Even if you are a new VA just starting your practice and do not have much experience, you can use descriptive words to take the spotlight off of being "new" and focus on other attributes, such as talented, qualified and accomplished. Rather than describing your business as new, you might say you are innovative. When creating your material, be truthful about who you are and what you do. Making false promises can lead to business ruin. As stated earlier, it is very easy to exaggerate your skills or knowledge in written format. Just provide an alternative way to say things.

Some phrases and words to consider:

1. For new VA's who are just starting out and do not have years of experience as a VA, try these words:

   - Talented
   - Qualified
   - Mastery of…
   - Talent for
   - Flair for
   - Skilled
   - Well-versed in…
   - Imaginative
   - Capable
   - Accomplished
   - Competent
   - Gifted

2. Do not say you are new in business, say this:

   - Innovative
   - Groundbreaking
   - Bold
   - Revolutionary
   - A Fresh Approach
   - Designed for today's…
   - A novel approach
   - Taking it to a new level

3. Being a new VA, you cannot say that your service appeals to many but you might say:

- Unforgettable
- Inviting
- One of kind
- Unique
- Memorable
- Pleasing
- Satisfying

4. Instead of older or established, try:

- Genuine
- True
- Original
- Actual

5. Even if your business is not big does not mean your scope of services or your commitment to customer service is not big. Try these suggestions:

- A host of
- Substantial
- Unlimited
- A multitude of
- Boundless

6. Being a Virtual Assistant you will obviously not have offices in every state but that does not make you any less convenient. To describe your availability, use these words:

- Fits your schedule
- Flexible
- Accessible
- Wherever you need it
- Whenever you need it
- Virtually anywhere

7. Instead of saying "better known", try:

- Distinguished
- Respected
- Notable
- Accomplished
- Outstanding
- High Reputation
- More and more......are discovering
- Recommended
- In demand
- Flourishing

8. Instead of saying "long-standing" try these:

- Practical
- Reliable
- Dependable
- Valid
- Trusted
- High Standards
- Secure
- A leader in...
- Competitive
- Quality-oriented

When creating your marketing material, use descriptive phrases that will enhance your image, help build a solid reputation and set you apart from your competition.

Suggestions are:

- We're dedicated to
- Devoted to
- We believe in
- We value
- We provide excellence
- We offer the added advantage of
- You will benefit
- Providing competitive services
- Here's why....
- Our dedication to....
- We serve

Chapter 3 – Summary

As you move forward through the next chapters and start creating the individual pieces for your marketing kit, remember that the written content is just as important as the overall look of your materials. Be clear on the message that you want to get across and be truthful in what you can provide.

Your Marketing Kit - Part I
Brochures, Flyers, Letterhead and a Sales Letter

Life is trying things to see if they work.
-Ray Bradbury

When creating your marketing kit, we suggest that you start with the most cost-effective and less time consuming items first. Above all else, enjoy yourself. Have fun with your creativity: experiment and be open to new things.

The first three items to consider for your marketing kit are three items that can be used in direct mailings to help promote your business: a brochure, flyer and sales letter.

Are these items effective in getting clients? Some individuals feel that these direct mailings are not as effective as advertising, other businesses that have used direct mailings are very happy with the end result. However, you will not know what works for YOU unless you try it.

Direct mailings will bring you a return rate of 1%, this does not seem like much. Think of it this way, if you send out 100 mailings and are hired by one client, this marketing method has paid for itself.

Before starting to create your brochure, flyer and sales letter, there are few items that you will need:

1. Desktop publishing software
2. Word processing software
3. Colour printer
4. Quality paper (preferably bond)
5. Envelopes
6. Stamps

As a Virtual Assistant you probably already have the software requirements for this project and if not, you should be looking into it. Desktop publishing and word processing software are widely used for clients. A good colour printer is also a necessity not only for your projects but for your clients as well.

Bond paper is a higher quality and more expensive paper than your everyday printer paper, however, the final product is superior. You want to make sure for your brochure that you are using a higher gauge (thickness) paper than you would for your sales letter.

Stamps and envelopes are a given for direct mailings. A #10 envelope will work fine for your mailings; if you want to be creative, try putting your logo on the envelope to give it more appeal. Stamps will be one of the more expensive items for this project but you cannot mail a letter without one.

For the highest success rate, more is better. If you can mail a minimum of 100 envelopes a month and increase this as your budget allows, your chances of someone who needs your service reading your material will increase as well.

Brochures

Brochures are an easy, cost-effective way to market your company. For professions such as Virtual Assistants where our clients are not easily contacted in person or by phone, a brochure provides a printed piece of material to grab the reader's attention.

Many small businesses believe that you need to get your brochure professionally printed – not so. You can create your brochure by using any of a number of desktop publishing programs available. The most common desktop program is MS Publisher™. Programs such as MS Publisher™ make creating a brochure simple and offer many different templates to get you started. We recommend that you use these templates for the overall structure and then modify to suit your company identity.

The tri-fold style brochure is the most common style of brochure and the style that we will be focusing on. This brochure easily fits into a standard #10 envelope and can be easily distributed by mass mailing. Tri-fold style brochures are also great when attending tradeshows and networking events.

Always make sure your content is proofread and there are no typographical or grammatical errors.

There are three important steps when creating a brochure:
1. Creating the content
2. Creating the design
3. Printing the brochure

Creating the Content

When creating the content for your brochure keep in mind you have six panels that need information. Selectively choose the content for each panel; we have made a few suggestions below:

Inside brochure – Panel 1
Include information on "What is a VA?" List the benefits of working with a VA.

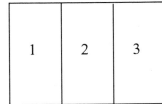

Inside brochure – Panel 2
Include information about your company, how long you have been in business, what your company can provide and why they should hire you!

Inside brochure – Panel 3
Include your bio and qualifications and consider including a picture of yourself as well.

Outside brochure – Panel 4
This panel will be the "cover" of your brochure. You should always include your logo, company name and tagline to stay consistent with your company identity.

Outside brochure – Panel 5
This is the "back" of your brochure. You should include a list of your services, along with your contact information or include your services on panel 6 and include only your logo and contact information on the back.

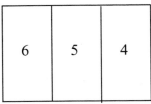

*Your contact information should include the mailing address, telephone and fax numbers, email and website addresses and cell phone (if applicable).

Outside brochure – Panel 6
This panel is the first page that your reader will see when opening the brochure. You may wish to summarize the reasons why the reader needs assistance – a lead-in to the concept of working virtually or include your services!

Other content you may wish to include in the brochure:

- Discount on Services
- Testimonials
- Coupon
- References

Creating the Design

When designing a brochure, keep in mind there are plenty of software programs available that have brochure templates included in them. These software programs are very easy to use and normally have "drag and drop" elements.

MS Publisher™ is an easy and effective program to use when creating your brochure and other marketing materials. If you do not already have MS Publisher™ installed on your computer, you can purchase it at your local retailer. It retails for approximately $100.00-$149.00 depending where you purchase it. This is a great program to have and will not only help you with your marketing materials but, as stated earlier, is a great service to provide to clients.

When designing your brochure, it is extremely important to maintain a consistent theme with the rest of your marketing materials. This directly establishes your company identity. Design elements to consider:

- Company Colours
- Logo
- Tagline
- Typeface (use the same style font)
- Use appropriate images (try not to use too many graphics; you want the focus to be on the content.)

Design Tip: Be very selective when using graphics or images. You do not want to overcrowd your brochure with inappropriate images. When considering images use more professionally geared graphics. Graphic suggestions: computers, clocks, a businessperson, diskette, telephone, calculator (bookkeeping), computer mouse, keyboard etc. Stay away from images such as animals, trees, insects, waterfalls etc. they are pretty to look at but have nothing to do with your services.

Printing the Brochure

The visual appearance of your brochure is extremely important so you want to ensure that you use high quality paper that presents your design and content well. Using the heaviest weight paper that you can find will give it a solid look: you do not want your brochure to be on flimsy light paper. Experiment with different coloured paper to give it a fresh look.

Printing your brochure in MS Publisher on your home printer can be a little tricky and you may have to do quite a few tests before you get it right. While testing, use your normal printer paper, do not waste your quality paper until you are ready. Once you have printed the front side, you will need to quickly flip over and insert the page so the back half will print. Try to ensure you do not have paper in your printer's paper tray or you will find that the other side will begin printing before you have a chance to flip over and insert the first half of the brochure.

Depending on the type of printer and the amount of colours you are using, you may have to change your printer cartridge often. Keep this in mind when designing your brochure. If you do not have the budget for replacing printer cartridges often, keep your colours to a minimum. Use just enough colour to stay consistent with your company identity.

Flyer

Perhaps the cheapest form of written marketing material is a flyer. A flyer is simply a brochure…simplified. Flyers are great for direct mailings or to market your services locally. A flyer is usually a single sheet of paper that you can distribute to local businesses or even hang up in your local grocery store. You will even find that many companies will distribute your flyer to households for a small fee. Obviously you are not guaranteed that there will be a return on this. As mentioned earlier in this chapter, even if you are able to get one client from this, your investment is returned.

The objective of a flyer is to get the word out about you and your business. By targeting businesses in your area, you are introducing them to what you do and the services you provide. Even if this is the only thing that you achieve…it is a great start. Word travels fast!

Creating the Content

You want to create content that is immediately going to entice the reader to read more. Use "hot words" that will grab the reader's attention: VIRTUAL is always an attention grabber so try to use that in your flyer.

Other hot words include:

- Cost-effective
- Efficient
- Effective
- Innovative
- Cutting Edge
- Discount
- Solutions
- Grow your business
- Support Services
- Make More Money
- Freedom
- Save Time

Creating the Design

Again, it is important that you are consistent with your company image: your logo, tagline and company name must be present on your flyer to create your company identity. Use the same colours and fonts that you have used for your other marketing material and again have fun when creating this piece. Use appropriate images: computers, telephone, diskette, and a businessperson, anything that will spark the reader's attention.

You can use either desk-top publishing or word processing software to design your flyer. Either will provide the design elements for you to create an impressive flyer. When printing your flyer, try to use a variety of coloured paper. Bright colours such as pink, yellow and blue will stand out.

Because you are working with limited space, you need to use a very simple and direct message. For example, on your flyer use the entire top half of the flyer for a one or two word headline to get the reader's attention so when they stop to look more closely, they will read the smaller print.

Your flyer should include:

- Your company name and logo
- Your tagline
- Company colours
- Full contact information
- What it is you do
- What you are offering
- The benefits of your service
- Why they should hire you
- A testimonial (if possible, not necessary)

Basic Flyer Design

Virtual Solutions

Administrative Solutions for your business

At Virtual Solutions, we provide top-notch administrative support for the professional. If you are looking for cost-effective, efficient and high-quality solutions for your business, call us today!

Have More Time
Save Money
Grow Your Business

Mention this ad and receive 25% off your first invoice!

VIRTUAL
SOLUTIONS

Primary Business Address
Your Address Line 2
Your Address Line 3

Phone: 555-555-5555
Fax: 555-555-5555
Email: xyz@microsoft.com

Letterhead

Your letterhead is the core of all your marketing material. For all correspondence you should be using your letterhead. If you used a graphic designer to create your logo, they will have provided you with the logo for your letterhead. If you have created your own logo, you can just insert into a blank document.

It is extremely important that you stay consistent with your letterhead. Your sales letters and any other marketing correspondence should be sent on letterhead. Using letterhead gives you a professional look and when corresponding with potential clients, this is precisely the image you want to reflect.

Your letterhead should be created in a word processor and be saved for future use.

Letterhead Content

It is imperative that your letterhead includes correct contact information; this goes for all your marketing material. If you move or change your number, make sure to update all your material.

Your letterhead should include:

- Company Name
- Your Name
- Title
- Address
- Phone
- Fax
- Mobile (if applicable)
- Email
- Website (if applicable)

Designing your Letterhead

To help you decide on the overall design of your letterhead ask yourself these questions:

1. Where will the logo go: top, left, bottom, right?

2. Do I want my information to appear vertically or horizontally? (i.e. across the top/bottom or down the side)

3. What quality of paper stock?

4. What colour of paper?

5. What colour of text?

By answering these questions you will have the foundation for your letterhead. Creating your letterhead is a simple project and should not take you very long. Again, you want to be consistent in your design and be happy with the end result.

If you are not comfortable designing your own letterhead and want to have this professionally created, there are a number of printers available to assist you. However, keep in mind that this service can be costly.

Design Tip: To ensure document stability, insert all design elements into the header and footer of your document. This will prevent images from shifting during transfer via email and ensure that the images show up on all pages of your document.

Sample Letterhead

Virtual Solutions

Administrative solutions for your business

123 Hope Place. Smithville. Ontario. L4P 3A8. P:905-555-1212 F: 555-4545 E: hope@roger.com

Sales Letter

A sales letter is a way to introduce yourself and your services to prospective clients in a personal way. The wonderful thing about writing a sales letter is you can think about it, control it and edit it. The opposite happens when you are speaking to someone in person or by telephone; you do not have total control over the communication. When you put something in writing, the reader has time to study and understand the message you are trying to communicate.

Written communication allows for:

- Reviewing tangible, physical information
- Using images, diagrams and other visual aids that may be helpful in getting your message out
- Representing your position when you are not there
- Opening the door for further conversation
- Viewing samples of your work

Sales letters are a way to communicate with prosepective clients at their convenience and yours. You want to approach your sales letter the same way as if you were writing a personal letter; you want to convey a real interest in the person to whom you are writing.

When creating your letter you need to decide how you will be delivering it. There are two ways in which to send:

1. Direct mail – An addressed envelope and stamp and it is on its way.
2. Email – They are cheaper and faster than direct mailings and you can write them any time of the day or night.

Either way is ideal, however with email, you must be especially aware of issues such as spam (unwanted emails). We suggest that these emails be a one-time mailing and even inform the recipient that this email is a one-time offering, and that you are conscious of spam issues. In some US states, there are laws regulating spam, but if you let them know you are introducing your service and you will not contact them again, you will not be breaking any laws.

Whether you plan to send your sales letter via email or direct mailing, we highly recommend that you use word processing software to draft your letter. Word processors have wonderful features to help you compose your letter such as letter templates, grammar and spelling checks and even a thesaurus to help you find that perfect word.

If sending an email, just copy and paste your text into a blank email and it is set to go; some basic formatting may be required to complete the look. When addressing your email, if possible use the person's name to give that personal touch. Make sure that you have a catchy subject line that will inspire the recipient to open and read it. Some suggestions are:

- Virtual Services
- <insert profession> Support (Real Estate Support, Coach Support, etc.)
- Administrative Freedom
- Supporting you with your business
- Virtually Assisting You

There are a variety of different phrases that you can use to peak the interest of the recipient.

Creating the Content

When composing your letter you want it to be as personal as possible. You want to be direct with your message and stay away from space fillers. Keep in mind that you are writing to introduce the reader to the benefits of using a Virtual Assistant and that YOU are the Virtual Assistant they should be hiring.

Items to consider when composing your sales letter:

- Include a personal greeting, that wishes them long continued business success
- Introduce yourself to the reader
- Let the reader know you understand their challenges (identify with them)
- Tell the reader how you can help them and the benefits they will receive
- Provide proof (testimonials, client references)
- Persuade the reader, offer a discount on services

There is an old saying around the concept of writing letters, say what you will say, say it, and then say what you said. This is not a bad approach: give people an overview of what is coming, then say it and then summarize what you have said.

One thing to remember is that we are talking about relationship-based marketing. We want to build relationships not only with existing clients but with prospective clients as well. The reader will want to feel as though you are talking specifically to him/her. Customize your letters for the individual. For instance, if the individual is a consultant, include something in your letter regarding their consulting business. This approach is much more time consuming, however it is much more effective.

> **Useful Key Phrases:**
>
> - Are you having trouble ...
> - This is why it is important to have ...
> - At X, we have the skills and experience to ...
> - Do you want to have more time to spend doing the things you love?
> - Do you want to start running your business instead of it running you?

Designing your Sales Letter

Being a Virtual Assistant, the administrative professional that you are, designing a sales letter will be a piece of cake. Remember: for consistency, use your letterhead with logo, company name and contact information.

There are two common styles of letters: a block letter and a modified block letter.

A block letter is the most widely used form for business letters and the easiest to prepare. You simply line up everything at the left margin, and type it single spaced with a double space between paragraphs. Do not indent.

The date line is typed two to six spaces below your letterhead and the address is below the date. The salutation is typed below the address and the letter will start two lines below the salutation. Very simple!

A modified block letter follows all the same rules as the block style except for a few modifications. The date is right aligned as opposed to the left and if you wish, you can right align the closing as well.

When deciding on the style of font to use, make sure it is easy to read and matches with your letterhead. Times New Roman and Arial fonts are the easiest of all fonts to read. Try to stay away from coloured text when designing your letter, it can be very distracting and not very professional looking.

Make the design of your letter aesthetically pleasing but simple – stay away from graphics other than your logo.

Email Letters

With the variety of email software and Internet providers out there, it is imperative to keep your email letter simple. You do not want complications with downloading graphics and file size interferring with your marketing efforts.

We recommend that you do not use attachments when sending your email letter. People become very nervous opening attachments from people that they do not know. With so many unknown viruses, there is becoming an increasing apprehension surrounding attachments.

Copy and paste your letter into the body of an email; use HTML or plain text. With HTML you can customize the look a bit by adding a little colour to your headings or even using a background image or colour.

If you do not have the time to personally address each email and plan to send out a large quantity, make sure to use a distribution list or the BCC coloum (Blind Carbon Copy) to hide the email addresses and protect the privacy of your recipients.

Sample Sales Letter

Friday January 24, 2003

Jonathon Smith
123 XYZ Street
Toronto, Ontario
M2K 4Y5

Dear Mr. Smith,

We hope your business is flourishing and you are achieving business success. We would like to take a moment of your time to acquaint you with our organization and the services we provide.

VA's R US is the one-stop source for virtual assistance. We offer a wide range of services:

- Bookkeeping, Client Invoicing, Accounts Receivable, Accounts Payable
- Desktop Publishing
- Document Preparation
- And all around general administrative support

As a principal in a growing company, you are taking care of all aspects of your business: client billing to accounting to scheduling and finally marketing. What percentage of your time are you actually actively growing your business? Wouldn't you like to spend more of your time doing the work you love?

We understand the challenges you are facing and have the answers you are looking for. We have a staff of fully qualified professionals to meet all your administrative needs.

"VA's R US have been a delight to work with: they're professional, reliable and wonderfully supportive. They are my administrative angels." -Susan Liptchitz

Contact us for a free personalized consultation with one of our client representatives to discuss how we can assist you in growing your practice!

We look forward to hearing from you.

Sincerely,

Jennifer Jones
President
VA's R US

PS: As a gift to you, here is a certificate for 2 free hours towards any project!

Chapter 4 - Summary

As you begin to develop the material for your marketing kit, remember to include as much of you into your material as possible; let your personality shine through all your materials. Be consistent with design in order to preserve your company identity.

Brochures, letterhead, flyers and sales letters are just the tip of the iceberg. There are so many ways for you to get your message out to your target audience. We will continue to work on these in the next two chapters.

Your Marketing Kit - Part II
Business Cards, Advertisements, Press Release, Newsletter

A creative mind is like a parachute - it only works when it's open.
-Merrill J. Oster

The next items to consider for your marketing kit are business cards, advertisements, a press release and a newsletter. These are not in any particular order, meaning if you want to start with creating a business card as your first piece of marketing material for your marketing kit, by all means do so.

You can create all of these items yourself for half the price of having them produced for you. However, we would recommend that, if budget allows, at least have your business cards produced professionally.

If you decide to create your own business card, you will need a few items:

1. desktop publishing software
2. business card stock
3. colour printer

When creating your press release or a newsletter, a word processor will be sufficient. As for your advertisement, read on.

All of these items are distributed differently as opposed to Chapter Four where direct mailings is the means of distribution. Each item in this chapter will be circulated either by hand, print or email.

Business Cards

Your business card will be the smallest piece of written material included in your marketing kit, yet it is one of the most important pieces. Your card conveys your identity.

Business cards are available in a number of styles to choose from, from the very boring to the more artistic. You may be surprised at the variety to choose from, more than you probably ever considered.

If you visit a printer you will find the selection overwhelming, and we do recommend that you have your cards professionally done. The cost is not as expensive as you may think. On average, you will be required to pay around $100.00 for 500 high quality business cards; 500 business cards will last you a very long time, unless of course, you intend to send a business card along with any of your direct mailings. In this case, you may want to order more.

If your budget does not allow for your business cards to be done by a professional printer, we highly recommend using a desktop publishing program such as MS Publisher™. As the same with brochures, MS Publisher™ provides a variety of templates for you to choose and you can modify as desired.

Creating the Content

As with all your marketing materials, make sure you include your company name, logo, tagline and all contact information:

- logo
- tagline
- company name
- your name
- title
- address
- phone
- fax
- mobile (if applicable)
- email
- website (if applicable)

Other content that may appeal to you:

- Print your services on the back of your card.
- You can include an inspirational quote or message on the back of your card.
- Include a discount on services.

Creating the Design

The possibilities for creativity are endless, experiment with designs and choose the one that best fits your company identity. Your printer will be able to help you with the selection process. If you decide to design your own cards, ask yourself these questions:

1. Where will the logo go: top left bottom right?

2. Do I want my card to be vertical or horizontal?

3. What quality of paper stock?

4. What colour of paper?

5. Do I want a photo or image?

6. What colour of text?

Other design options that you may want to consider:

- Use a folded business card
- Have your card printed on coloured background stock
- Ask your printer for raised lettering

Design Tip: Although vertical business cards are unique, try to stay with a horizontal design. It will fit better in most business card storage systems. As well, choose an ink colour that will photocopy or fax well.

Printing your business cards

If you have decided to create your own business cards, make sure to check the printing options in your desktop publishing software. Normally these software programs will give you the stock number that you will need in order to print effortlessly.

You will most likely end up paying approximately $20.00 for the business card stock at your local business supply center. There will be a large selection so if you can, purchase a couple of favourites and try them.

Keep in mind that if you are using an ink jet colour printer, you may find that your text may bleed a bit; it may not have that crisp look that a professional printer can provide you.

Sample Business Card

Supporting Today's Entrepreneur

Janet Smith

President

123 Terrace Drive
Toronto, Ontario
M3H 4T7

Phone: 555-555-5555
Fax: 555-555-5555
Email: janet@vasrus.com

VA'S R US

Advertisements

If you are advertising your services in the newspapers, Yellow Pages or any other print media, you are buying space. Normally your ads will be designed for you by the advertising publication. However, if you know what you want and can design your own ad, you are more likely to attract your ideal clients. If deciding on print advertising, having an ad already created that you can show the ad designer at the publication will make the experience easier for you and the designer.

Remember to include your logo, business name and tagline for consistency.

Creating the Content

Unlike your flyer and brochure, you have limited space when creating an advertisement. Your ad is not effective if it does not grab the attention of the reader. You want make sure that, regardless of the size of your ad, you include a standout headline.

When you are creating an ad, the headline is the most important element. It must entice the reader to read the ad. Most of the time, people will glance through ads only stopping to read the ones whose headlines interest them.

When writing the content for your ad you need to speak to people's interests or needs. Headlines should convey the benefits of your service, rather than highlight you.

Hot words to use in your headline include:

• new	• avoid	• announcing
• now	• at last	• 100%
• free	• finally	• unique
• amazing	• breakthrough	• save
• guarantee	• stop	• discount

It is much easier to create your ad if you have some sort of model to start from. This requires you to do research. Buy a copy of the publication you plan to advertise in and review all the ads that are in the publication. Find at least five ads that you found grabbed your interest. Pay close attention to the words in the ad that you found attracted you to the ad.

There are so many different ways you can approach headlines:

- Direct - tell the reader what you offer right away
- Indirect - trigger curiosity
- Demand - tell the reader to act now
- Testimonial - share benefits experienced by others
- Reason - list the reasons why they should read further

Designing your advertisement

Depending on your budget and the advertising rate of the publication, your ad may measure 2X2, 3X3, 4X5, 5X5, etc. Contact the publication to confirm the dimensions of the ad. You will also need to ask about the submission format; some publications require your ad to be in an image format such as .jpg, .gif or .tif files.

You can create these image files by using a variety of software programs available such as PaintShop Pro, Adobe™ Illustrator, Adobe™ PhotoShop, etc. Keep in mind these programs can be costly and in some cases, without training, may be difficult to use. Remember what you do for yourself, you can do for potential clients.

Whatever the size of your ad, you want to ensure that your headline stands out. For larger ads your headline should take up at least one-quarter to one-half of your ad. For smaller ads, use a larger font and differentiate by making it bold.

Do not try to cram in a lot of information, it will be difficult to read and not very pleasing to the eye. Again, MS Publisher™ offers ad templates that can help you get started.

As a low cost alternative to purchasing a new program, print out a high resolution paper copy of your ad, scan it into your computer and save it as a jpg, or tif file!

Sample Advertisements

Size: 2 X 2

Virtual Assistant Services

VIRTUAL SOLUTIONS

Administrative solutions for your business
Visit us at
www.virtualsolutions.com

Tel: 555 555 5555

Size: 3 X 3

Virtual Solutions

Top-notch VA services for the professional. Offering administrative solutions for your business. Word-processing, data processing, desktop publishing and much more!

Call us today and receive 10% off your first invoice
555-555-5555
Visit us at:

www.virtualsolutions.com

Benefits to you:

- **NO payroll**
- **NO taxes**
- **NO training**

Size: 4 X 5

Top-notch VA services for the professional. Offering administrative solutions for your business. Word-processing, data processing, desktop publishing and much more!

VIRTUAL SOLUTIONS

Call us today and receive 10% off your first invoice
Tel: 555 555 5555

www.virtualsolutions.com

Press Release

A press release is the main tool used to generate publicity and is a great way to announce the launch of your practice. A press release summarizes important points of your story that may be of interest to the press. The objective of a press release is to receive coverage in the media. By creating an effective press release and finding just the right individuals to send it to, you may find this will lead to newspaper, magazine and even some media features such as radio or television. There is never any guarantee that your press release will be picked up, but if it is, it could turn out to be a once in a lifetime opportunity for you.

Creating the Content

In order to write a good press release, there are some common features that you will want to include:

1. **Contact information** - it sounds simple enough but make sure that it is featured at the top of your release.
2. **Immediate Release** - at the top of your release include instructions for when the news can be released to the news. Most often you will want to simply notify the media that the news is "For Immediate Release."
3. **Headline** - make sure to include a headline in capital letters. Your headline should include a verb. This makes the headline appear "active."
4. **Dateline** - the very first sentence in your press release should include the date the release was sent, and the city/state or province where the release originated.
5. **5 W's plus how** - who, what, where, when, why and how must be used.
6. **Use one or more quotes** - present meaningful comments.
7. **Three pages or less** - ideally one page is preferred, however if your release runs over, do not print on both sides.

Some topics for your press release include:

- Launching of your practice
- New services you are offering
- Major clients you have obtained
- A new certification you have earned
- A seminar you are giving
- Anniversary of your company
- Client success stories
- Awards you were given
- Memberships into associations

Designing your Press Release

All you need is a word processor and you are ready to go. Make sure your press release is on 8 ½ x 11 inch white paper. Use 1½ inch margins and if possible use 1½ inch spacing.

Sending Your Press Release

There are three main ways to distribute your press release:
1. Distribute it yourself - mail, email or fax your press release to media outlets.
2. Use a news distribution service - an electronic service that distributes time-sensitive material to the media.
3. Hire a PR professional - can distribute your press release for you.

It is totally up to you how you want to distribute your press release, however, we suggest that you consider distributing it yourself – the most cost-effective method out of the three.

Start by researching publications you want to target. Consider starting locally as a test and if you are happy with the results, start sending your press release to other publications that you feel would be suitable. Contact the editor of your local paper and introduce yourself and tell them about your business. As a Virtual Assistant, many local papers will be interested in the way in which you do work…virtually.

As well, the Internet is a fountain of information, just do a search on business magazines, business publications, small business magazines, etc., and you will find the contact information readily available.

Once you have found the publications you wish to target, consider emailing your press release or faxing your information directly to them. Faxing and emailing will get the information to them more quickly than mailing.

If you do not hear back within a few weeks, follow up to see if they received your information and if they have any questions that you could answer.

Sample Press Release

NEWS RELEASE
For Immediate Release

For more information contact:
Samantha Smith
Samantha@virtualsolutions.com

VIRTUAL SOLUTIONS LAUNCHED

April 22, 2002 – Samantha Smith, from Lake View, Ontario is announcing the launch of her company Virtual Solutions. Virtual Solutions is a company providing Virtual Assistant Services to clients throughout North America.

By utilizing today's technology, Virtual Assistants are providing innovative solutions to small businesses, home-based businesses and entrepreneurs world-wide. A fairly new profession, but one that has seen a dramatic growth over the past two years, Virtual Assistants are the answer to companies world-wide who are looking for administrative support but do not want or need the services of on-site support.

Samantha Smith, owner/operator of Virtual Solutions lives in a small town in Ontario yet provides services to clients who live literally miles away. The distance, however, is never a problem since the growth of technology has paved the way for professions such as Virtual Assistants. All work assignments are received via email and items such as word processing, database management, and desktop publishing are the primary requests from clients.

"Working with Samantha has been a wonderful experience. Being a home-based business, I am unable to have the necessary administrative support available to me until now. Virtual Solutions is really just that: a wonderful solution to any business who needs administrative help!"
Joanna Anyone – JA Consulting Ltd.

For more information, contact:
Samantha Smith
Virtual Solutions – www.virtualsolutions.com
123 Hope Drive
Lave View, Ontario
L8N 9I2
Tel: 555-555-5555
Fax: 444-444-4444
media@virtualsolutions.com

Newsletter

Creating a newsletter is a great way to get the word out about what you do. Newsletters are casual, friend-to-friend communications that deliver useful information to your recipients and build relationships.

By creating a newsletter you will be:

- Building credibility and reputation
- Having frequent communication
- Providing useful tips that build client confidence and loyalty
- Delivering news about your business
- Sharing success stories
- Providing industry information

Be prepared that newsletters only work when they are distributed consistently. Writing a newsletter is a commitment to your readers which means you will be writing your newsletter for a very long time.

One of the first things to consider is how often you plan to distribute your newsletter, weekly, bi-weekly, monthly, quarterly, etc. We suggest that you start with a monthly newsletter; this gives you plenty of time to prepare each newsletter, without getting overwhelmed.

Creating the Content

In order to begin creating the content you must ask yourself what is the purpose of your newsletter. Is it to communicate with clients, enhance your reputation, or to share tips on productivity?

Whatever the reason you need to be clear before you can offer it to readers.

Your newsletter will need to contain valuable information for the recipient, not just promotional information about your services.

Some tips to keep your readers...reading:

- Keep your stories short
- Show your personality
- Always include your contact information
- Include a brief table of contents
- Newsletter title, date and edition for easy filing
- Funny anecdotes to lighten up the newsletter
- Invite reader responses

Designing Your Newsletter

As well as being the cheapest to send, an email newsletter is also the easiest to design. Preferred by most Virtual Assistants, e-newsletters are easy to format and distribute to readers.

You have two format choices when sending an e-newsletter:

1. Plain text - Simple, but not aesthetically pleasing
2. HTML - Offers more creativity

If you choose to use plain text, you can create your newsletter in a word processor and then copy and paste into a blank email. Add some minor formatting and your newsletter is ready to be sent.

For a more creative newsletter, we suggest you use an HTML-based newsletter. These HTML newsletters can be created by using your email program and having the mail format set to HTML or you can use a web developing program such as MS FrontPage™ to create a professional looking newsletter.

Either way, HTML offers the most design options.

Hard copy newsletters

Some individuals prefer a paper-copy; by far, however, this is the most time consuming and expensive way to produce a newsletter.

Again when designing a hard copy newsletter, do not try to create one from scratch – use templates available in a desk top publishing program. There are a variety of styles and themes to choose from and will allow for you to modify to suit.

Distributing your newsletter

Building a newsletter subscription list will take time, in fact it may even take years to build your subscriber base to 100- 200 people, but it will happen.

Make it easy for people to subscribe to your newsletter.

- Add a link to your website and have available information about what your newsletter is all about.
- Find e-newsletter directories on the Internet, where you can list your newsletter for free.
- Sign up friends and family, they would appreciate hearing from you.
- Ask existing subscribers to forward onto friends who may be interested.

Chapter 5- Summary

Both business cards and advertisements are considered common elements when marketing, however, not everyone starting a VA practice is aware of the marketing potential of press releases and newsletters.

When creating your marketing kit, remember that it is solely up to you what you want to include in your kit. The items you include will be directly affected by time, money and your interest.

Marketing Kit - Part III
Client Information Package

Forget everything except what you're going to do now, and do it.
-Will Durant

Your client information package will be one of the most important pieces of your marketing kit. How you represent yourself and your ability to produce top-quality services will directly affect whether or not your business will be successful.

A client information package incorporates all the information a prospective client would need to know about you before they hire you. All packaged neatly and conveniently for the prospective client, a well-designed package will include an introduction letter, company profile or biography, services offered, fee schedule and more.

You will be able to create your client information package using a word processing program but there will be other items you will need:

- Your letterhead
- Adobe Acrobat™ or a PDF generator (for e-version)
- Quality paper and portfolio (for hard-copy version)
- Colour printer
- 10x13 mailing envelopes (for hard-copy version)
- Stamps (for hard-copy version)

It is not necessary for you to have an electronic (e-version) and a hard-copy version of your client package. If cost allows, we suggest that you try to have both available. You may have a prospect that would prefer to receive your information via standard mail.

If you are a new VA or even an established VA, it is very important that the materials you give your clients represent yourself in the best possible way. By providing your prospective clients with professional, attractive documents with intelligent and flowing text, you are already showing the prospective client what you are able to do.

Reasons to use a Client Information Package:

1. **Marketing tool**
   We have already established this is a unique and vital piece for any VA's marketing kit. The reason is that your client information package has the same effect as word of mouth. If you pass on your information to a prospective client and they like what you have done, they will pass it on and the next person will pass it on, and so on and so on. You get the idea.

2. Establishes identity

By having a client package, you are establishing your company identity and helping it get noticed. By placing your information package on your company letterhead, it adds credibility to you and your company.

3. Offers something tangible

By having an e-copy or hardcopy version of your client information package it offers the clients something tangible. When working in a virtual environment, it is nice to have materials that a client can print out and look at or be sent via standard mail.

4. Gives clients an Idea of your skills and personality

Believe it or not, your prospective clients will learn a lot about you and your skills by viewing your information package. You will want to put as much of you in the package as possible.

Creating the Content

There is no right or wrong to creating the content for your client information package. You can include the information that you deem important to your business.

Here is a guideline to help you get started.

Your client information package may include the following:

1. Letter of Introduction
- Initial piece of the information package
- Introduces you and your services to the potential client

2. Services Offered
- Includes all the services you are offering

3. Fee Schedule
- Covers your rate, payment options, etc.

4. History of the Organization/Your Biography
- Includes information about you, your experience, skills, etc.

5. Testimonials/Reasons to Use a VA
- Testimonials from past employers or benefits of using a VA for general interest.

6. Client Questionnaire
- This piece will assess your prospective client's needs.

Letter of Introduction

The letter of introduction offers a personal greeting to the client, it allows for the personal touch. This letter will give you the opportunity to thank the prospective client for his/her interest in you and your services.

Your letter of introduction should include:

1. **The name and address of the prospective client**
   If possible, always address your introduction letter to the prospective client by using their full name. Some clients may contact you via email – in this case you may not have their mailing address but you should have their name. Use it in your introduction letter to achieve a personal touch.

2. **Start with a friendly greeting**
   Do not be too informal here – "Hello" or "Dear" are always appropriate.

3. **Provide an introduction to the issue of why they may need your services.**
   Ask yourself why clients are contacting you, why is it that they need your services, what you can provide them and touch on this in your letter.

4. **Explain why a VA is the answer for them.**
   Use "hot words": efficient, effective, no payroll, no taxes, no space, self-starter, highly-skilled, dependable, and committed.

5. **Explain why YOU would make the perfect VA for them.**
   Draw on your past work experiences, your unique abilities, personality traits.

6. **Ask them to complete your Client Questionnaire.**
   It is important that they complete this form; explain to them in your letter that it will help facilitate the relationship, give a deeper understanding to their needs.

7. **Close with a positive note for follow-up.**
   I look forward to working with you, if you have any questions please feel free to contact me.

Sample Letter of Introduction

Mr. John Smith
At- Home Consultants
123 Villages Way
Ville, ON J0J 0J0

Dear Mr. Smith:

Thank you for contacting VA's R US for more information on our services

Running a small business can be a challenge and often paperwork becomes a chore. You are trying to build a business – who has time for paperwork?

You probably do not have space for a desk and certainly cannot afford to hire a full time assistant: - that's where Virtual Assistants comes in. We work from our offices and provide all the support you need to clear the paperwork off your desk.

Having worked as a personal secretary for a number of vice presidents at Canada's Fortune 500 companies, my experience is invaluable. Consider me YOUR personal secretary – but also a partner: we'll work together to build your business while providing you with more freedom.

Please take a moment to complete the Client Questionnaire, the last page of this document. It will help me to understand where I can help you!

Please do not hesitate to call me if you have any questions.

Sincerely,

Sue Sams
President

Company Profile/Biography

By including background information about you and your company, you are providing necessary information regarding your skills, work history and accomplishments to the prospective client. Be honest about your credentials, skills and accomplishments; do not over-exaggerate anything.

It may contain:

1. Your Vision Statement

Example:
VA's R US is Canada's pre-eminent provider of virtual assistance, dedicated to excellence in administrative services.

2. Your Mission Statement

Example:
VA's R US provides total customer satisfaction through reliable, efficient and cost-effective services.

3. Your Core Values

Example:
At VA's R US, we will be:
- *accountable and efficient*
- *proactive and progressive*
- *respectful*
- *customer-focused*

4. Your competitive advantage

Example:
VA's R US professionals have more than 25 years of experience providing administrative solutions to businesses in the GTA.

Writing a company profile or biography seems simple, but most people find it difficult writing about our own successes. To help organize your information, use the questions below as a starting point.

1. How long have you been in business?
2. Why have you started the business?
3. What special skills do you possess?
4. List your major accomplishments.
5. Why are you the perfect VA?

Sample Company Profile/Biography

About VA's R US

I started VA's R US in 2000, after many years in the corporate world, providing secretarial support to the vice-presidents of some of the top Fortune 500 companies in Canada. When downsizing affected one company, I was asked to continue to provide support to the ex-vice presidents/entrepreneurs from my home office – a perfect solution for a bad situation.

Working in the corporate world provided me with training and experience in the latest applications of Microsoft Office; Word, Excel, and PowerPoint are my specialties. I am strategically driven and love to partner with my clients to help them grow their business.

Professionalism and accuracy are my credo. I am a perfectionist at heart and take great pride in my work and, therefore, in yours. Who could ask for anything more?

VA's R US provides total customer satisfaction through reliable, efficient and cost-efficient services.

Services Offered

The description of services will list the services that you offer and offer a brief description of what each service entails. When listing your services, it is important that you only list those services that you do well. You have to be 100% confident in your skills before you can offer them to a client. Make sure that you not only list the services but the subsections of the services so that the prospective client understands all that it entails.

If you have a niche market, list the services that would cater to them.

Some services you may include on your service list are:

BOOKKEEPING
Invoice clients
Track expenses
Monthly financial reports
Budget preparation
Cash flow projection

CONTACT MANAGEMENT
Manage client base
Schedule meetings and
appointments

DATABASE MANAGEMENT
Customized structure
Personalized reports
Bulk mailings
Mass emails
Purchase mailing lists

DESKTOP PUBLISHING
Flyers
Brochures
Newsletters
Letterhead
Logo Design

DOCUMENT PREPARATION
Excel
Word/WordPerfect
PowerPoint
Letters
Reports
Training manuals
Proposals

EMAIL/VOICE MAIL SERVICE
Standardized responses
Screening
Timely follow-up

MARKET RESEARCH
Mailing lists
Web Links
Publishers
Associations

MEETING MANAGEMENT
Conferences
Trade Shows
Video Conferences
Audio Visuals

Sample Service Description

At VA's R Us we provide customized solutions for all your administrative needs!

BOOKKEEPING
Invoice clients
Track expenses
Monthly financial reports
Budget preparation
Cash flow projection

CONTACT MANAGEMENT
Manage client base
Schedule meetings
Schedule appointments

DATABASE MANAGEMENT
Customized structure
Personalized reports
Bulk mailings
Mass emails
Purchase mailing lists

DESKTOP PUBLISHING
Flyers
Brochures
Newsletters
Letterhead
Logo Design

DOCUMENT PREPARATION
Excel
Word/WordPerfect
PowerPoint
Letters
Reports
Training manuals
Proposals

Fee Schedule

The fee schedule will provide the reader with information on your fees and payment options. Rather than simply listing a rate, you should provide a rationale as to why the rate is reasonable.

1. **Goal is to provide a reliable and effective service.**
   Make sure your prospective clients are feeling that by hiring you they would get their money's worth.

2. **Consider making the rate negotiable.**
   This is very important – always be flexible with your fees. Make sure that you are available to all clients of every budget. You do not want to take a huge loss but keep in mind that if their budget is a little tight now, once their business grows, so will yours. You may wish to incorporate a three or six month allowance of reduced rates and then review these rates again at this time.

3. **Consider offering a discount to ongoing clients.**
   For clients who will be using your services for more than 15-20 hours a month, offer a reduced rate. Deducting $5.00 from your standard rate will give them a feeling of value. As you know, a feeling of value adds to client loyalty.

4. **Be SURE to include what the rate does NOT include.**
   Make sure that you list the extras such as couriers, faxes, postage, long distance telephone calls, stationery, etc. that your rate does not include.

In addition to listing your fees, the fee schedule should include additional information. It should contain:

1. **Billing schedule**
   By providing your billing schedule, your prospective client will get an idea from the start when your invoices are issued. We suggest that you consider billing some of your clients in the middle of the month and some at the end, so you have money coming in twice a month.

2. **Payment options**
   It is important that you list your payment options: credit card, cheque or cash. If you want to accept credit cards, you will need to contact your bank and open a merchant account.

3. **Fee structure**
   Have a clear fee structure for your practice; decide early on how you will be charging for your services.

Sample Fee Schedule

Hourly Plan
We understand the need for temporary assistance!

This plan is for those who need short-term or occasional support, who do not require the services of a Virtual Assistant regularly.

$30.00 per hour for all services

Invoice will be supplied with accurate accounts of all hours billed. Expenses will be charged separately.

Retainer Plan
For our clients who require services on a regular basis, we offer a lower hourly rate of $25.00 (*this is our standard rate, yet negotiable).

Fee Structure- Retainer Services
20 hours per month at $25.00 per hour = $500.00 per month
(5 hours a week)

40 hours per month at $25.00 per hour = $1,000.00 per month
(10 hours a week)

Additional expenses incurred such as couriers, facsimiles, postage, long distance telephone calls, will be charged separately.

Billing Schedule
Payment is due upon receipt of invoice. Invoices are sent on the 15th and the 30th of each month. We accept payments by cheque, VISA and MasterCard only.

Testimonials

Providing testimonials gives potential clients a sense of your legitimacy. If you do not have any clients, consider contacting former employers and asking for a written reference.

The testimonial should be:

1. brief
Your testimonials should be one paragraph if possible. If you receive a testimonial from a client, ask if you may edit the content if it is too long.

2. specific
When you request a testimonial, ask if they could be specific in what it is that they are really happy about, a specific service, personality trait, etc.

3. signed
If your client is unable to sign it, ask if you can use their name and website address in your testimonials.

As you get more clients, ask them for testimonials.
The six month mark is a good time to ask a client for a testimonial.

Do not get carried away.
Provide only two or three testimonials in your information package. Remember, you do not want to overwhelm with too much information. If you have a website, incorporate all of them on it.

Sample Testimonials

Here's what our clients are saying!!!

Working with VA's R US has been wonderful – it's like having another me around! We work together on projects and they help to keep me organized.
Jane Smith
Coaches Corner

The staff at VA's R US have been very professional and responsive to my needs. Their attention to detail has helped me to grow my business and provide satisfaction to my clients.
Joe Anyone
On the Top Consulting

The best business decision I've made was hiring VA's R US. They have become a valuable member of my team and provide insight and feedback that has proved invaluable. My success is a tribute to their great service.
Olivia Newbrook
MOMS R US

Reasons to Use a Virtual Assistant

If you do not have testimonials, another item to consider is a general interest piece on the reasons to use a Virtual Assistant. Not every client who comes to you will know exactly what they are looking for, so help them along by offering a list of benefits or reasons to use a VA.

They can include:

- No need to purchase equipment or furniture

- No need to provide a physical space

- No need to worry about payroll, deductions, etc.

- Minimal training

- Pay for project time as opposed to "office time"

- Access to administrative professionals

Sample Reasons to Hire

Top Ten Reasons to Hire VA's R US

1. You no longer need to spend valuable time on tasks you do not have time for.

2. You do not need to provide a physical workspace.

3. You do not need to provide costly equipment for your VA to use.

4. You do not need to deal with payroll, taxes or benefits.

5. You can have the time to focus on the more important issues of your business.

6. You have the freedom to work on growing and improving your business skills, knowledge, and relationships.

7. You have a partner to share or "bounce" ideas.

8. You have the flexibility to assume new, challenging opportunities.

9. You have a peace of mind knowing that the details are being handled.

10. You are finally able to run your business instead of it running you.

Client Questionnaire

A Client Questionnaire will help you to better assess the needs of the potential client. The well-designed questionnaire will focus the client on exactly what functions the VA will perform.

Questions should include:

1. **Basic contact information**
   Name
   Company
   Address
   Telephone number
   Fax number
   Email address
   Website (if applicable)

2. **A brief description of the current administrative support being utilized.**
   This question will give you an idea if a prospective client has used a VA in the past or is presently using another means of administrative support.

3. **Current administrative challenges**
   This will give you a clear picture of the problems he/she may be facing and allows you the opportunity to find solutions to the problems.

4. **What would the perfect VA do for the client?**
   This question is specifically asking them to picture their ideal VA.

5. **Current hardware/software being used**
   This is very important for compatibility issues. Because you are working virtually, it is important that you have all the information in order to work together effectively.

Additional tips to help you create a Client Questionnaire:

   a. Keep it short – one page only
   b. Be sure to include your return contact information
   c. Make it user friendly
   d. Consider using "check boxes" or Yes/No responses

Sample Questionnaire

Client Questionnaire

CONTACT INFORMATION
Name, Address, Tel, Fax, Email

_____
_____
_____
_____

ABOUT YOU
Tell me a little about your
business.

_____
_____
_____
_____

WHY A VA?
Tell me about a typical workday
and how I can help. _____

_____
_____
_____
_____
_____
_____
_____

WORKING TOGETHER
Tell me about where you would
like to be in 5 years.

_____
_____
_____

PLEASE CHECK THE SERVICES YOU ARE CONSIDERING:

☐ Bookkeeping

☐ Voicemail/Email Response

☐ Document Preparation

☐ PowerPoint Presentations

☐ Special Project Support

☐ Appointment Bookings

☐ Contact Management

☐ Other _____

Do you currently have an administrative support person?

__ Yes __ No

PLEASE RETURN BY FAX TO: 590-590-5905

Designing Your Client Information Package

Once you have created the content, the final step will be the overall design of your client information package.

- Use a word processor to create your client information package; keep it simple in design.

- Be sure to put your letter on your company letterhead (your letterhead should incorporate your logo, company name, tagline and contact information).

- Be consistent with the font style throughout the document. Select a font that is easy to read (Times and Arial are the easiest on the eye).

- If possible, have your signature scanned in so you can electronically sign your introduction letter (adds a personal touch).

- Stay away from too many graphics – not only will it clutter the content, it will increase the document size and, if delivered by email, will increase download time.

Closing the Sale

Statement of General Terms and Conditions

Another sub-section of your client information package is a statement of general terms and conditions, otherwise known as a contract. Once a client has hired your service, you would then discuss the terms of the working relationship. A contract will outline the items such as confidentiality, payment policy and ownership.

When creating any contact, it is always a smart business decision to have a lawyer review your contract.

It should contain:

1. **Statement of Confidentiality**
    Be clear that you offer 100% confidentiality. You will be viewing various documents and information regarding your client's business, and he/she will want to know that their information is safe with you.

2. **Independent Contract Status**
    Outline the relationship of the parties.

3. **Pricing and Payment Policy**
    Include your agreed upon rate as well as the date of the month they will be billed as well as any penalties for late payments.

4. **Reimbursement of Expenses**
    State what your rate does not include. This is the same information that you included in your fee schedule.

5. **Ownership of work**
    Any work that is not accepted by the client is yours.

6. **Statement of Acceptance by Client**
    Have your client sign your agreement and fax back to you.

7. **Line for Name of Client, Signature and Date**

8. **Billing Information**
    Include a space for your client to provide full contact information. You will need this for your billing records.

Sample General Terms and Conditions

General Terms and Conditions

Confidentiality
It is understood that in the performance of duties by VA's R US we will obtain information about both the client and their customers/clients, and that such information is confidential. We provide a 100% confidentiality policy to all our clients.

Independent Contractor
VA's R US are hired as independent contractors and are not eligible for any benefits programs or tax withholding obligations on the part of the client.

Payment & Pricing Policy
You will be billed an hourly rate of $30.00. Invoices will be submitted once a month and payment is due upon receipt of invoice. A 2% per month late penalty charge will apply to all delinquent accounts.

Reimbursable Expenses
The following expenses incurred on behalf of the client will be billed at direct cost:

a) Long distance charges
b) Courier charges
c) Mailing costs
d) Travel time
e) Travel expenses if site visit is requested
f) Specialty paper
g) Specialty software

Ownership
Any rejected plans, ideas or designs remain exclusive property of VA's R Us.

Acceptance by Client

By signing below, client hereby agrees to these general terms and conditions.

_____
Name of Client

_____   _____
Signature of Client   Date Signed

Please provide full contact information below for billing purposes:
Full Name:
Mailing Address
Phone:
Fax:
Email:

Distributing your Client Information Package

Hard copy version

When sending your materials via standard mail you will need the following:

- Presentation Portfolios (these can be purchased at any office supply store)
- Bond paper (use high quality paper when printing out your information package)
- 10 x 13" envelopes for mailing
- Avery Mailing Labels (we suggest 02163 shipping labels)

Make sure your package represents you well!

Email Version

When sending your materials via email you will need the following:

- Adobe Acrobat 5.0 or later software program or PDF capabilities such as online creation of PDFs at Adobe's website.
  Adobe enables you to create PDF documents (Portable Document Format) which will ensure that your package will retain the formatting. This software is a program that you will use on client work as well so it is worth the investment.
- An email program

REMEMBER: When creating your welcome package with the intention of sending an email version, make sure that the size of your file is not too large for people to download.

Chapter 6 - Summary

Your client information package should represent you well. A properly crafted package will not only provide important information to prospective clients about you and your services, it will also provide them a sample of your work. Your package will give them a clear indication of your writing, editing and design skills.

Creating a client information package is an asset for the content basis of your company website. The biography, service description and testimonials can now be incorporated into a website, which will be the focus of our next chapter.

Marketing Kit Part IV
A Website

What is now proved was once only imagined.
-William Blake

The last item for your marketing kit cannot only be one of the most expensive but the most complicated. We do not mean complicated in terms of creating content and design, but more so in understanding the behind the scenes items that go into building a website.

Domain names, search engines and web hosting are all items that directly relate to the production of your website, and in creating a formidable marketing tool for your business.

You will find that not all Virtual Assistants have a website and some VA's do not feel the need for an online presence. However, a majority of the VA community recognizes the potential a website can offer. A website offers you an opportunity to market your practice globally.

In order to begin your website, it is important that you plan for it. Be aware of what you like and do not like when it comes to design and content elements. Begin by researching other websites; make a list of all the sites that you like and the reasons why they appeal to you.

Another point to consider is hiring a web designer. We highly recommend that if you do not have the skills to create a functional, professional looking website that you hire someone to build it for you. As with all your marketing materials, you want to convey the image of your professionalism. By hiring an experienced web designer, you will be introduced to a whole new world of web elements which you may not have even thought about.

This chapter is filled with useful information to help you plan and build your website and ultimately, your online marketing presence.

Getting Started - Things you need to know

There is plenty to do when building a website. One of the first steps is to decide on your domain name.

Acquiring a Domain Name

Practically speaking, your domain name (web address) is the core of your Internet identity, your online brand. Your customers will remember this name and use it to find your website and your services. Since no two parties can ever hold the same domain name (web address) simultaneously, your Internet identity is totally unique.

Technically, a domain name (web address) is an addressing used for identifying and locating computers on the Internet. While computers use Internet Protocol (IP) numbers to locate each other on the Internet, people find them hard to remember. Therefore, domain names (web addresses) were developed to permit the use of easily remembered words and phrases to identify Internet addresses.

For example, the domain name (web address) microsoft.com represents Microsoft's website. When you type microsoft.com into a web browser or send e-mail to someone at microsoft.com, the Domain Name System (DNS) translates microsoft.com into the IP numbers used by the Internet and connects you to microsoft.com.

What are the Components of a Domain Name?

Top-Level domains

A top-level domain (TLD) refers to the suffix attached to Internet domain names. The most common top-level domains used on the Internet are .com, .net and .org.

Country Code Top-Level Domains

Two letter top-level domains, such as .ca .uk, .de and .jp, are called country code top level domains (ccTLDs) and correspond to a country, territory or other geographic location. The rules and policies for registering domain names in the ccTLDs vary significantly from country to country and may be reserved for use by citizens of the corresponding country.

How to Choose a Domain Name

When first setting up a business, most people will register a domain name that mirrors exactly the name of their company. It is important that your domain name incorporates what you are doing. This becomes a large factor when you are submitting to search engines. For example, as a Virtual Assistant you may want a domain name like the following (these domain names are samples only):

http://www.virtualexecutiveassistant.ca
http://www.virtualofficeassistant.com
http://myvirtualassistant.com
http://GinaVA.com

Another important piece is choosing the extension that goes along with it. Below is a list of commonly used domain name extensions and what they mean:

.com – commercial business
.ca – Canada
.net – network organizations
.org – non-profit organizations
.gov – government agencies
.edu – educational institutions

Recently .tv, .biz, .name, .pro and .info have been released as domain name extensions.

Registering Your Domain Name

There are many sites on the web where you can register your domain name. You must first do a search on their site to see if the domain name you want is available. Domain names are given on the first come first serve basis and will cost you approximately $30.00 CDN a year.

Go to any search engine and do a search for Domain Name Registration and hundreds of companies will be located.

Web Hosting

Every website needs a host; this is the company that provides the server where your site will sit. There are plenty of web hosts available to help you select the right hosting package for you. Depending on the packages available, the cost can start anywhere from $15.00 CDN a month to $100.00 CDN per month.

When choosing a hosting company, keep these points in mind:

1. **Look to the future** – As your customer base and revenue grows, your site may require the addition of server-side scripting, eCommerce and database support. Make sure your host is big enough to accommodate your future needs, as well as your present ones.

2. **Know what you need** – do not empty your bank account paying for services you do not need.

3. **Prompt service and performance** – The popularity of your site will be directly affected by your host's level of service. Slow load times due to an overburdened server will send your customers elsewhere. No matter how renowned your host, technical problems will occur. As such, demand 24-hour, 7 days-a-week technical support for all your applications.

4. **Security** – Ask for a detailed description of the hosting company's security protocols. They should provide adequate protection from everyday denial-of-service attacks and the various hacks and cracks that will be attempted on your server. Make sure that your host is responsible for upgrading and maintaining these measures.

5. **Get what you pay for** – When shopping for a host, you will find that they vary widely in terms of target and pricing. Some hosts skew their servers to accommodate many small sites, while others prefer to take on fewer, high-volume sites. Be sure to strike a good balance between price and volume flexibility.

6. **Do not commit right away** – Treat your web host like you would treat any other supplier for your business. If they cannot provide the service and reliability you need, why keep them? Their competitors will be happy to have your business.

Creating the Design

When you surf through the World Wide Web, you occasionally find a web page that grabs your interest and causes you to examine it further. You may even bookmark a really good site so you can return to it quickly and easily. However, if you come across a website that is poorly designed, unattractive or does not work properly, you find yourself quickly moving on.

There are many design factors at work that influence our perceptions of web design. We can look at a page for the first time and form an impression in less than five seconds. If it is a good impression, we may venture to look closer, if not we will move on.

Creating and designing an effective web page primarily begins with what appeals to you. Some of us may not even know what we like or what appeals to us. That is why every great website starts out by doing a lot of research.

You want to convey your company identity – include your logo, tagline and business name.

Understanding Your Online Presence

1. Target audience – what may appeal to one group may be totally inappropriate for another. If you do not understand your target audience, there is no way you can effectively prepare to create a website.

2. Purpose – the three basic purposes of web pages are to provide information, to entertain and to enable exchange. Decide the purpose of your site.

3. Style – essential to good web design. Well-designed websites project a look and feel that helps to convey a positive image of the person, business, organization or product being represented.

Website Organization

When organizing your website, it is important that you have a clear picture of the outcome. You will want to structure your site for easy navigation, flowing content and an overall pleasing look. Have a clear idea of the number of pages you want, the content of those pages and how they connect to one another.

Site Navigation

Since a website is a collection of related documents, you need a navigation system that allows visitors to find the information they are seeking. Visitors want to easily navigate to find the necessary information, document, service, product or entertainment.

Before we can successfully accomplish this, we need to know how all the pieces fit.

Your Home Page

A homepage is the gateway to the site. Its first priority is to clearly communicate the name and subject matter. On the home page, there must be a clearly defined way to access the other content on the site. These other pages should have hyperlinks that take the user directly to them.

Once beyond the home page, there are several models for organizing navigation; we will focus on only one, the simplest to understand.

The hierarchical navigational model is an easy model to use when creating a simple and effective website. This model will help you become clearer on the pages that you would like to include in your site and how your navigational buttons or hyperlinks will link to each existing page. There is no limit to the number of pages that a site can have – this is an individual preference.

Here is a basic model to start you on your way:

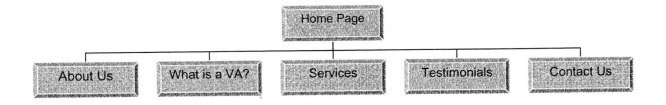

About Us
This page tells the visitor about you and who you are.

What is a VA?
Explains more about the VA profession to visitors who are unfamiliar with the term.

Services
You may want to include a detailed list of the services you provide and the benefits of your service.

Testimonials
This is an optional page. A testimonial page is a great way to display comments from happy clients.

Contact Us
Include a page that includes all your contact information: address, telephone, fax, cell phone numbers and email address.

Design Tip: Using Images

You want to use images sparingly on your site. The number of images and size of image files directly affect the download time of your page. If someone has to wait five minutes to view your site, they will quickly move on. Discuss images with your web designer to ensure your images will not affect a speedy download.

Creating the Content

Home Page

Your home page is the introduction to the rest of your site. You want to make the content easy to read, appealing to look at and not in the least bit overwhelming. Use "hot words" when creating the content for your home page such as "efficient", "cost effective" and "innovative" to really grab your visitor's interest. Try to stay away from unnecessary multimedia add-on's such as music.

Some content you may want to include:

- Welcome your visitor
- Introduction to your company
- One or two nice graphics (you do not want to overdo it)
- Easy to use navigation links to the other pages of your site
- Contact information at the bottom of the page

About Us

This is the page where you want to tell all your visitors and potential clients about you, your skills, education, and credentials – any information you feel would interest those visiting the site. Keep in mind these visitors are also potential clients.

- Why are you in the profession
- What qualifies you
- Why they should hire you now
- What skills you possess, any niches
- How long you have been in the profession
- Any affiliations
- For the personal touch, include a picture of yourself.

What is a VA?

Not only for the VA profession but for any newer profession, it is important that your visitors understand what it is you do and are able to provide them. Not everyone who visits your site will know what a Virtual Assistant is or does. Explain to them as clearly as possible:

- Brief introduction to the profession
- Benefits of using a VA
- Reasons to use a VA
- How VA's work
- Include an appropriate image

Services Page

This page allows your visitors the opportunity to find out exactly what services are available to them if they hire you. This page would be a great place to include the benefits.

- List your services
- Provide a brief description of each service
- Explain the benefits
- Provide an email link on the page so they can contact you quickly and conveniently with any questions
- Include an appropriate image

Testimonials (optional)

Your testimonial page should include brief comments of praise from existing or past clients. Your testimonial page should include:

- Brief comments
- Clients' name
- Clients' company name
- Clients' website (if applicable)

Contact Us

This page should include all contact information. You want to make it as easy as possible for potential clients to contact you with questions or comments. Remember to include your country as well. Because we work virtually, it is important that potential clients know where you are located.

- Include name, phone and fax numbers
- Email addresses
- Mailing address (your preference)
- Office hours

Hiring a Web Designer

We strongly encourage you to seek out a web designer when making the decision to create a site. Any reputable designer will take the time to listen to what you want and offer advice and suggestions on how to make your site a success.

We suggest that you research and interview at least three different web designers and get quotes.

Some questions you may wish to ask a prospective web designer are:

1. How long have you been designing websites?

2. Can I see your portfolio?

3. Do you work hourly or flat rate per project?

4. Do you also provide maintenance and at what charge?

5. What is your turnaround time?

6. Can you provide flash, java, java script?

7. Can I contact past clients as references?

Chapter 7 - Summary

Your website will be the global marketing tool in your marketing kit. You want your site to reflect your professionalism, creativity, innovation and skill as a competent writer. It is important that you also understand how other elements work such as domain names, search engines and web hosting so you can effectively market yourself through your website.

Online Marketing

The Internet allows information to be distributed worldwide at basically zero cost.
-Bill Gates

The World Wide Web is a very powerful marketing medium. Nobody knows this better than Virtual Assistants. As VA's, we are accustomed to the ongoing marketing messages delivered to us in the form of websites, pop up ads and email messages.

Although the web is just one marketing method, it is the one medium where we can incorporate all of the major marketing categories from Chapter One. Customer service, sales, advertising, research and much more can be integrated online.

There are three main types of online marketing:

1. **Your web presence (your website)**
   Your website is an interactive brochure that provides useful information to your clients, the press and the casual visitor. However, your website will not market for you until you get people to visit it.

2. **Other people's web presence (their website)**
   Placing reciprocal links to directories or association directories will help to get people to visit your site. Placing links on larger, better-known sites will increase the traffic to your site.

3. **Your email**
   Email is an outgoing form of communication and, therefore, considered to be marketing. Email marketing can consist of your company newsletter, a sales letter or even a personal note to an existing client.

Another marketing type, however it may be indirectly, is search engine usage. You can use the web to gather information about your prospective clients and your competition. Online searches allow you to find important information regarding individuals, companies and, in some cases, will even provide you with the contact information to send your marketing material. As you know, the web is a fantastic research tool.

Why Online Marketing?

Very simply, doing business online allows for communication and relationship building, and is a cost-effective way to get your marketing message to your target market.

Nine Advantages and One disadvantage to Online Marketing

1. **Cost-effectiveness** – In some cases, online marketing can cost you nothing except time. You can get information to your customers without paying the cost of printing or postage.

2. **Speed** – You can send or post updated information to your clients and prospects immediately.

3. **Self service** – Prospective clients can visit your website and help themselves to the information as opposed to waiting for you to send it to them.

4. **Interactive** – Online marketing allows prospective clients to leave feedback.

5. **Abundant information** – The use of graphics, video, sound and text provide an information-rich marketing medium.

6. **Exposure** – Online marketing exposes you to a large and diverse audience that otherwise you may not have been able to target.

7. **Global** – Online marketing is international, and you have immediate access to the global market.

8. **Open 24/7** – Prospective clients can find you 24 hours a day, 7 days a week.

9. **Community** – Online marketing creates a sense of community and by using newsletters, emails and your website, you can strengthen relationships.

Disadvantage

1. Sometimes people assume that all they need to market their service is a website – this is not so. The VA approach to marketing is about building relationships with others. You can use online methods to enhance your relationships with clients and prospective clients, however, your website cannot do it all for you.

Marketing Your Services Online

Your website is a very large part of marketing your services online, however, you can do other things to enhance your website's marketability and much smaller things aside from your website.

1. **Website Links:** There are a variety of sites that you can "team up" with and offer reciprocal links. This means that you will put a link on their site and vice versa. This not only will provide you with more traffic to your site, it also tells the visitor that the site endorses your site and thinks that it is worthwhile for them to visit it. Do a search for "link exchange" and you will notice exchange sources from many countries.

   When you have found the right person or company with whom to exchange links, consider having their site directed to a new window as opposed to them leaving your site completely. The objective is to keep your visitors on your site.

2. **Discussion lists and forums:** Discussion lists and forums provide an opportunity for you to build relationships and provide free advice. There are a variety of online forums devoted to small business; join one and offer your expertise.

3. **Advertising on Other Sites:** You will find plenty of advertising space available on the web. Research some professional directories that target your specific audience. For example: if you want to market your services to real estate agents, do a search for real estate directories; you will find that most directories will offer banner ads. Of course, as with all advertising, it does not come for free. Before spending a lot of money, make sure it is worthwhile. Ask for website statistics such as the number of visitors during a specific period of time.

4. **Encourage Referrals:** An innovative way to encourage referrals is to create a way for visitors to easily refer you to others. Have a link on your site that enables a visitor to email your website link with a message that says "Check this out". If you want to get really creative, have a post card or image that a visitor can send just by filling out their email address.

5. **Web Pages:** Presentation goes a long way, as discussed in Chapter Seven. There is definite value in a well-designed and aesthetically pleasing web page.

6. **Content:** Try always to have fresh content. Add new features, links, articles and other items to your site to keep it interesting to the visitor. The more frequently you update your material, the more often repeat visitors will come by to see what is new.

7. **Search Engines:** Being listed on some of the top search engines is one of the best ways to be found. Search engines are one of the primary ways that Internet users find websites. A website with good search engine listings may see a dramatic

increase in traffic. We will discuss search engines in greater detail later in this chapter.

8. **Meta Tags:** Meta tags define your web page and website to the outside world. You can declare the title, keywords and description which will help your placement in search engines. This is very important for all websites and you should pick your meta tags wisely. Do not repeat your keywords too much.

   Sample Keywords for a VA site
   Virtual Assistant, VA, Virtual Assisting, office support, administrative assistant, executive assistant, word processing, database management, "Your Name".

   Sample Description for a VA site:
   VA's R Us provides professional, high-quality virtual assistant services to clients world-wide.

9. **Emails:** Sending your sales letter via email is another great way to market online. Make sure to keep them as individual as possible. Type in the person's name and customize the email to target that particular individual. Some individuals may ask you not to contact them again, but you will find that others will respond positively to your personal approach.

10. **Email Signature:** Just as if you were writing a letter and signing it, use the same concept with email. Create a signature which includes your name, company name, title, contact information and website address. Make sure to include this signature on all correspondence. Depending on the email program that you use, a signature template may be built in and you can program it so it automatically appears every time you send a new message.

Search Engines

Search engines are one of the primary ways that Internet users find websites. A website with good search engine listings may see a dramatic increase in traffic. Yahoo, Google.com, Google.ca (Canada), Canada.com, Lycos and HotBot are all well-known search engines.

How Search Engines Work

There are two types of search engines that gather their listings in extremely different ways.

1. **Crawler-Based Search Engines**
   Crawler-based search engines, such as HotBot, create their listings automatically. They "crawl" or "spider" the web and people search through what they have found. If you change your web pages, crawler-based search engines eventually find these changes, and that can affect how you are listed. Page titles, body text and other elements all play a role.

2. **Human-Powered Directories**
   A human-powered directory, such as Yahoo, depends on people for its listings. You submit a short description to the directory for your entire site or editors write a description for sites they review. A search looks for matches only in the submitted descriptions. Changing your web pages has no effect on your listing.

When creating your site, it is important that you speak to your web designer or, if doing it yourself, do some research on site placement among search engines. There is never any guarantee that you will be listed on a search engine, but by learning more about search engines and optimizing your placement, you will stand a better chance of being listed.

Search Engine Submission

There are many companies that will submit your site to 3,000+ search engines for a fee. Keep in mind there is no guarantee for placement. You may pay your fees and find that it does absolutely nothing to boost your placement or you may be the rare individual that benefits from this process. Of the 3,000 search engines that most of these companies submit to, there is only a handful that people actually use.

Manual Submissions

If you are on a budget, you may consider manually submitting your site to search engines. This is free although very time consuming. There are some places that you can submit to 20 sites at a time for free. Please be aware that by using these sites, they will ask you for an email address before they will submit for free. Five minutes later, you will be bombarded by emails from various companies. If this is not a problem for you, simply delete the emails and go on with your day.

Fee-Based Submissions

There are certain search engines such as Yahoo and Looksmart that you can manually submit to, however, you will be charged a fee from $49.00 to $200.00 US. This fee is only for them to review your site and does not guarantee submission.

Pay-Per-Click and Bidding on Keywords

Some search engines, such as Google and overture.com, let you create your own listing and keywords. You are ranked depending upon the amount of your bid for that particular keyword. Highest bidder wins! This can be beneficial because depending what your budget is, you can be ranked within the top 10 listings on that particular search engine.

Example: If you bid $0.25 on the keyword "Virtual Assistant" and that is the highest bid you will be ranked #1. Now you only pay 25 cents each time someone clicks on your link.

What Search Engines Look For When Ranking Your Site

Every search engine is different. However, there are a few key points to remember when creating your site. Implementing these factors may help the ranking of your site with the major search engines:

- Search engines often change their requirements. Updating your site and resubmitting it periodically (no more than once a week) will help to maintain your position.

- There are programs like "Web Position Gold" which tell you exactly what each search engine is looking for. When you purchase the program, you are entitled to updates which keep the information current.

Although some search engine requirements conflict with others, following these guidelines may help you improve your overall rankings:

- Choose a domain name with your main keyword in it.

- List keywords and descriptions for EVERY page, however overuse of your keywords may have a negative impact on your rankings.

- Incorporate your keywords into the title of the page.

- Have your keywords in the top section of the body of text on your page.

- Use keywords as links, e.g. if your keyword is "virtual assisting", link those words to another appropriate page on your site.

- Use ALT tags over graphics with your keyword in it. Alt tags are alternative text the browser may show if an image cannot be displayed or disabled by the user.

- Do not fill your entire page with the same keyword; use it only when appropriate.

- Some search engines take into account how many links to your site are on other sites, so consider a link page. You can add related links to your page in return for the same on someone else's site.

- When possible, manually submit your site to the search engines. Some do not accept auto submissions so if that is all you use, you may miss out on some important search engines.

- Some search engines rank you on how long the visitor stays on your site. So if you are listed fourth and you can keep most visitors on your site for a long time, you may move up in rank.

- Consider fee-based and pay per click search engine listings if your budget allows.

- Although some search engines tell you only to submit your home page, try submitting other pages as well. This could increase the number of listings that come up for your site.

- Do not submit more than your home page to Human Powered Directories, (Open Directory, Yahoo, etc.), and do not submit your site more than once a month. They generally have strict rules about spamming and can reject your site for that reason alone.

Be patient when submitting your site to the search engines; it can take months to even show up and moving up in rank can be even more difficult. Your best chance is to submit regularly and to update your site with new content periodically.

Successful Online Marketing

In order to be successful at online marketing, you need to be open to new ways to get your message in front of your audience. Always keep in mind that the VA approach to marketing is based on relationship building.

It is very easy to get caught up in the convenience of sending a generic mass email to a distribution list but before you do this, ask yourself if you are building relationships.

There are other ways to build relationships with individuals you do not know, ways in which you can open that door.

Offer something of real value

This real value could be as simple as providing them with more information about what you can do for them. For example, if you are not quite sure if the individual you are emailing would be interested in your services...ask them.

Start your email off by simply stating "I'm not sure if this service would be appropriate for you, but if it does interest you, I would be happy to provide you with more information."

For the individuals who request more information, this is where the beginning of relationship building takes place. It is imperative that you send the information right away. As well, this would be a great time to offer a possible discount on your services, helping to build that relationship and offering more real value.

Once you begin developing the relationship, add these individuals to your newsletter distribution list and other communications that express your personality. This will allow them to get to know you better and build trust.

Trial and Error

With all forms of marketing, whether it be via the Internet or more traditional methods, success comes by testing to see what works. It is all about trial and error. With all the options available to you on the web, it is a great place to see what works and what does not.

Tips for testing:

- Start with the cheapest and work up. Try all the free methods of advertising on the web before paying.

- Do not be afraid to try new things. Be confident with what you are offering and explore new ways to get your message out.

- Build an online community. Start an e-group or discussion list that is directed to office productivity, tips or advice.

- Track the results. You need to know what is working and what is not, to prevent you from focusing your energy on a dead end.

- Research and more research. Do not sign up for anything until you are quite confident that you will reach your target market.

- Before advertising on any site, ask for a full rate card. Find out the number of visitors on a daily basis and ask for any demographics before you sign up.

- If you are going to exchange links, make sure that the site that you are exchanging with will represent you well.

Chapter 8 - Summary

Bill Gates summed it up best when he said, "The Internet allows information to be distributed worldwide at basically zero cost."

There are so many ways to market your practice online, being open and experimenting with new methods is the key to success. Remember that regardless of the method, the outcome should be focused on relationship building.

Advertising and Free Publicity

In order to sell a product or a service, a company must establish a relationship with the consumer. It must build trust and rapport. It must understand the customer's needs, and it must provide a product that delivers the promised benefits.
-Jay Levinson

With each ad you buy, you take your chances. Advertising is the mass media, paid approach to marketing, and in most cases the least effective way to market your services. It is the least personal and the most expensive and does not build relationships.

Is advertising worth it?
The first thing people think of when marketing their services is to advertise. For well-known service professions such as dentists, accountants or plumbing, advertising offers a service that most people recognize. This is not always the case with Virtual Assistants, the majority of the readers are not going to fully grasp the concept....yet.

We are not trying to discourage you from advertising; it is your dollar. However, before you do, it is important that you research your choice of advertising and stick to your budget. It is very easy to get blinded by the thought of more business.

Types of Advertising

There are so many ways to advertise and plenty of people who will sell ads to you:

- Newspapers
- Magazines
- Online
- Yellow Pages
- Newsletters
- Radio
- Television
- Billboards

Even your own vehicle can be a means of advertising your services.

Newspaper Ads

For most small businesses, advertising in a local paper is their medium of choice. If you talk to a variety of small business owners who advertise their services in the newspaper, you will find that there are many differing opinions on what works.

Some people will tell you to place small, witty ads on the regular basis while others are firm believers that larger ads placed less frequently is the way to go.

Again, it is trial and error, unfortunately with advertising it is your hard earned money that may be spent with no return. So how do you proceed?

1. Understand your target market and try to make an educated guess about the days and sections of the paper they are most like read.
2. Create an ad that presents what the prospect wants — refer to Chapter Five for creating your ad.
3. Research how advertising works by talking with ad sales people at the paper. This will allow you to prepare the best schedule possible for ad placement.

Advantages of newspaper advertising:

- **Wide coverage:** Newspapers reach many readers within certain areas or regions.
- **Targeted segments:** Advertisers can place ads in the travel, lifestyle, sports or other segments which better match target market profile.
- **Absorb readers:** Readers expect to see ads and spend time reading them.
- **Predictable timing:** Most readers will read the newspaper promptly upon its delivery.
- **Minimal planning:** You normally do not need to give much advance notice when placing an ad.
- **Flexibility:** There is plenty of flexibility when placing an ad. Most newspapers sell ad space by the column inch, so you can buy as small or as large a space as you want.
- **Cost:** Not extremely cost-effective, however, it is among the lowest of all mass media ($500 and up).

Now the disadvantages:

- **Read quickly:** Most papers are usually read quickly and then discarded.
- **Limited targeting:** You will pay to reach the full circulation even if a small portion of the readership fits your target profile.
- **Cluttered environment:** Although newspapers try to balance news versus ads, the clutter of stories, images and ads is unavoidable.
- **Print limitations:** You may be limited to black and white images and line illustrations.

Scheduling your ad

When to schedule your ad is as important as the information within your ad. The fact is, however, only about three percent of people open their papers from Monday through Friday. You will find that Tuesday will have the most readers being this is normally when the grocery and department store flyers are inserted.

For best results, consider these two tips:

- Place your ad on the day that you feel makes the most sense for your market and your message.

- Advertising in the Sunday paper does cost more however, it is widely distributed. Sunday papers usually sell 10-50 percent more than weekday papers. The reason for this is the reader has more time to read the paper on a Sunday than during the week.

Ad placement

Where your ad is placed does not attract readers, your ad itself will attract readers. You will find that some people adamantly believe that the right-hand page of a newspaper is the most desired placement. It may be the most desired but not necessarily the most effective. There has been no confirmed proof that ads on the right hand side get more attention than those on the left hand side of a newspaper.

Instead of worrying about where your ad is being placed, focus on the content and the overall look of your ad. Ask yourself if your ad is carrying the message you want it to carry and is it an attractive design that will pull in the reader.

Think about the following when deciding on ad placement:

- If you are determined to have a specific placement, make a request. Most newspapers will do their best to help you.

- Ask about special rates for ads in specific sections of the paper that may target your specific market. For example, if you plan to assist Real Estate agents, ask if there is a special rate for the real estate section.

Classified Ads
In terms of cost, advertising in the classified section is the cheapest. There are two types of classified ads:

Display ads: Larger ads featuring headlines, images and logos, these are available in all sizes and have a better chance of standing out than a small print classified ad.

Small print: These are the tiny ads you see that are normally arranged in categories and do not stand out as well as the display ads.

Print Guidelines

Whether you plan on advertising on the front page of the business section or in a small print classified ad, the guidelines are the same:

- Always use a headline. You can accomplish this even with a small classified ad. Have your headline in capitals and bolded so it stands out.
- Make sure your ad talks to your target market.
- If placing an ad in the classified section, place it in a variety of categories if you feel it will attract more than one interest area.
- Include your contact information. Regardless of size, you need to make it very easy for prospects to contact you.

Magazine Ads

If you have a big budget, magazine advertising is for you. For most of us who have limited advertising budgets, magazine ads are sometime unreachable. To place a full page ad in a magazine such as Time, it would cost close to $200,000 – you could buy a house for that much money.

Magazine ads such as Time, Entrepreneur and Canadian Business cater to companies such as IBM, Microsoft, HP, etc. These companies have advertising budgets in the millions of dollars, it is no wonder that small businesses cannot compete.

However, there are smaller publications that serve particular business or interest groups where you can place an ad for a fraction of the price of larger, more well-known magazines.

Research Magazines

There are thousands of smaller magazines available to advertise in, all you need to do is find them. The Internet is the best place to start.

- Do a search for small business magazines, you will find that quite a few directories will show up.
- Start a list or database of the magazines that you feel would target your market.
- Call these magazines or if they have a website, visit it and obtain a rate card.
- Ask for the demographics.

You will find that these smaller magazines will be more apt to work with your budget than some of the larger magazines.

Scheduling your ad

When scheduling your magazine ad, consider the following:

Frequency: Make sure that your budget allows for you to place your ad in the same magazine at least three times over a six month period.

Crossover readership: If you would like to advertise in a single month, place your ad in three magazines with similar reader profiles. This is called "crossover readership" between publications.

Response time: Unlike newspapers, reader response to magazine ads is not immediate.

Ad size: Full page ads will get noticed the most; if your budget does not allow full pages (in most cases it will not), consider using one-third page ads.

Design: Unlike newspaper ads, where most of us can design it ourselves, magazine ads will require you to hire a professional designer to create an ad that will be able to compete in the magazine environment.

Magazine ad representatives: Work with the magazine ad rep and build a relationship. Explain about your business, your goals with the ad and your budget.

Yellow Pages and Business Directory Ads

You will find as a VA, most of your prospects will not be looking for you in the Yellow Pages. As a matter of fact, at the time this book was being written, the Yellow Pages did not even have a heading for Virtual Assistants.

Advantages to Yellow Page advertising:
- Six out of ten consumers say they do not have a preference when turning to the Yellow Pages
- Those who read the Yellow Pages are ready to hire your services
- Twenty-four hour accessibility
- Geographically specified

Disadvantages:
- Majority of prospects will not look in the Yellow Pages to hire a VA
- Yellow Pages does not have advertising for Virtual Assistants
- Your ad remains the same for an entire year
- Too much advertising clutter
- Your ad will have to stand out to get results

As stated in earlier chapters, a majority of your clients will come from referrals and word of mouth, however, if you want to list your services in the Yellow Pages, here are a few tips:

Where to place the ad:
If a prospective was looking for your services in the Yellow Pages, where would they look first? With the Yellow Pages, you can have your ad placed in more than one category, however, it will cost more.

Size of the ad:
Big is not necessary in the Yellow Pages. Do research and see what your competition is doing. You will find that in many of the categories, the most established businesses run the smallest ads.

Colour or Not:
Again, research what your competitors are doing; is it necessary to choose a colour ad to compete with the other ads in your section? If you decide on colour, make sure you read the rate card carefully, colour charges mount up quickly.

Choose the right directory:
Before spending your money on any directories ask for distribution information. Find out exactly how many people receive the directories and how often.

What should your ad include?
As with all your print ads, your headline is one of the most important elements. Other information which may be valuable to the reader include:

- Listings of services
- Benefits of services
- Special qualities
- Length of time in business
- Professional endorsements
- Full contact information

How should your ad look?
If possible, hire a designer to create an ad that matches your company image. Try to stay away from the directory designers in order to create a unique image for your ad.

Television and Radio Broadcast

Television and radio ads are one of the most expensive ways to market your services. We will not spend a lot of time on advertising through TV and radio, because of the cost associated with it and is way out of budget for most VA's.

However, there are some ways you can take advantage of what television and radio can offer. This would be more in the area of publicity rather than advertising, however it is free.

Publicity is one of the best marketing tools for services and the best way to get publicity is to have a regular schedule for contacting media.

For radio and television, the best way to contact media is to start compiling a media list. You will need to do a lot of research to get the name of those individuals in charge of programming at the TV or radio stations. Start by sending out press releases to local TV and radio stations and see what the response is.

If you are comfortable, call a few program managers and tell them about what you do and what is unique about it.

Target those stations that you feel would best represent you to the viewers – small business shows and career shows are great places to start.

There is no guarantee that you will be called for an interview or to be a guest on a show, but if you do, watch out…the response can be overwhelming.

Free Publicity

One of the first things most people think of to get regular publicity is to write an article for a newspaper, newsletter or magazine.

Being featured as a regular writer in a newspaper or magazine can be surprisingly hard to achieve unless you know someone or have a connection.

However, here are a few suggestions to get your name in print…at no cost to you!

Letters to the Editor

Believe it or not, letters to the editor is the second most read part of the paper. People like to read what other people are saying and thinking.

One of the best ways to get your letter published is to add something extra to an article that was already printed. For example, your local paper runs a story about the challenges of working from home. This would be a great lead-in for you to comment on the effectiveness of working with a Virtual Assistant. There are plenty of stories that would enable you to add your own little piece of expertise.

Create your own news

Begin writing articles and tip sheets for newspapers, magazines and newsletters. In the PR world they call these tip sheets the "ten commandments." These are a one-page sheet of tips from your field, for example: Top Ten ways to work with a VA, Top Ten ways to be more productive, etc.

Giving talks and workshops

Giving talks and workshops is an ideal way to get publicity and promote your services. You could put a workshop together on a variety of topics such as:

- Small business productivity: Use a Virtual Assistant
- How Virtual Assistants can help your business succeed
- The Virtual Assistant: Secretaries of the new millennium
- Work from Home? Enjoy the benefits of working with a VA

There are a variety of angles – the objective is to appeal to prospective clients.

Not everyone is comfortable speaking in front of groups, however, there are some ways to overcome this phobia:

1. Understand that it is normal to be nervous, and prepare yourself for this…move ahead. Remember, the participants are interested in what you have to say or they would not be there.
2. Do establish eye contact. Look at the audience and establish eye contact with a variety of people. You will see them smile and this provides an instant connection and comfort.
3. Tell your story. Give examples or real stories: how you got into the business, challenges you have experienced or accomplishments you are proud of achieving.

Key Elements to a Good Presentation

There are four key elements in delivering an effective presentation:

1. Content
2. Sharing
3. Excitement
4. Customizing

Content

When creating the content for your presentation, decide on three clear points that you want to get across to the audience. Under these three items, develop specific details. By focusing on clear and simple points, your audience will be able to understand your presentation and the elaborated information.

Sharing

Give a little bit of yourself to the audience. Share interesting stories about you, your background, even your childhood if it can be incorporated into your presentation. By providing real stories, your audience will be able to relate to you and your topic and remember what you are saying. Sharing good stories is always memorable.

Excitement

Reflect your excitement and passion for your topic. If you show excitement for your topic, it becomes infectious and your audience will begin to feel your emotions. There is nothing worse than listening to a presentation where the presenter has no passion or excitement.

Customizing

Customize your presentation, even if it is just a few lines for each audience that you present. It could be as simple as changing the introductory remarks. The best way to customize your presentation is to know the people to whom you are speaking. If possible, mingle before the presentation.

Most importantly, do not read the content; the worst way to present a workshop is reading word for word from sheets of paper or worse cue cards. Your audience will respond better if you let your presentation flow naturally, not forced.

To get your presentation or workshop noticed, place an ad in your local paper and to generate some publicity, invite a local reporter to attend.

Chapter 9 – Summary

Advertising is impersonal and the least cost-effective way to marketing your practice. It does not incorporate the ideal marketing methods such as building relationships and providing superior client service. However, it is the easiest way to market your services, sometimes even easier than the more personal approach.

Networking & Building Community

Nature gave us one tongue and two ears
so we could hear twice as much as we speak.
- Epictetus

Even Virtual Assistants need to learn the fine art of networking. Though you work from the comfort of your home, it is imperative that you begin to develop your "networking circle". You will find that a networking circle is a very powerful tool when marketing your practice. Networking is not only about how many relationships you can build, but it also introduces you to individuals and resources that may help you in your business.

There are two options for networking:

1. **In person networking events:** Networking events such as your local chamber of commerce or small business group are great ways to meet local business people within your community. Remember that the members of these organizations are small businesses…your target market.

2. **Virtual networking meetings:** You will find plenty of virtual meetings that you can attend simply by dialing into a conference line. Quite a few Virtual Assistant associations and networking communities have regular networking calls that you can attend as part of membership. This is a wonderful way to meet your fellow VA's and expand your community.

Networking is not the easiest task; if you are somewhat shy and introverted, it will be challenging to put your apprehensions aside and introduce yourself to new people. However, it will all be worthwhile in the long run.

Most of us already have networking circles that we are not even aware of. We have networks of friends, networks for schools we attended or schools our children attend. There are neighborhood networks, sporting event networks, job networks and even networks within our free-time activities.

Your best contacts will already be a part of your existing network; they are just waiting to be found. One of the best ways to market your services is to have the people in your existing networks market for you. Word of mouth and referrals will be the key to your success.

The people in your network not only provide word of mouth and referrals but will also provide you with your social needs or be a source of positive thinking, encouragement and support. Networking is a great way to deal with the isolation of working from home. Approach networking as a social event, having fun and meeting new people, not as a way to get as many referrals as possible. Expect nothing and you will reap the rewards.

Top Ten Tips for Successful Networking

1. **Find out WHO the person is.**
   Approach networking like a big treasure hunt. Find out as much as you can about the other person. Make the goal in all your conversations to connect rather than impress. The more interests you have in common with the other person, the easier it is to connect and remember each other and build a relationship.

2. **Keep track of who you know.**
   At each in-person networking event, you will come home with a bunch of business cards. Make sure you have an effective way to manage all your contacts. Use a database to organize contact information, special notes, and where you met the contact.

3. **Network everywhere.**
   Use every opportunity you have to meet and network. Try to schedule time each week to attend networking events in your area.

4. **Project sincerity.**
   Be authentic, let people know who you are and be honest. People will be observing you as well.

5. **Prepare a 30-second elevator speech.**
   Develop a 30 second introduction that clearly states a benefit for the person you are meeting. Your introduction is a statement that lets them know how you can help them or someone they know. Practice this introduction so you can say it in your sleep (more information on your 30-second elevator speech later in this chapter).

6. **Listen more than you talk.**
   The art of great conversation is being a good listener. Ask questions that draw out other people. When you talk, you are not learning anything new.

7. **Ask for referrals.**
   You do not necessarily need to come right out and ask someone you just met to provide referrals for your business. Ask in a way that lets them know that you are not just thinking about what you can get from them. For example: A*sk people what would be a good referral for them.* This will encourage them to reciprocate and ask you the same question.

8. **Give a lot and first.**
   Give to your network at every opportunity. The best way to create a network of people who want to do things for you is to do things for them. These things can take the form of just about anything. Offer to assist with a project, be a resource for them or it may even be as simple as being a sounding board.

9. **Use your own networks.**
   Your own network consists of friends, family and colleagues. Do not hesitate to ask for business from your existing networking circles. Most people would rather do business with someone they know and trust.

10. **Always expand your network.**
    Continually adding new contacts and resources to your database is a way to be a resource for others and increase the opportunities of reciprocal business.

More tips for Successful Networking:

- Know what it is you want to accomplish before attending any networking events.
- Always have business cards in your wallet, pocket or purse.
- Keep track of your success. After each event make a list of what you learned and how the event helped you.

Top 10 Networking Myths

1. **Networking is about what you can get from others.**
   Networking is all about building relationships and what you can do for others.

2. **If you know a lot of people you have a strong network.**
   This is true is some sense, however, the old saying "it's who you know" does come into play.

3. **Networking is about schmoozing and collecting business cards.**
   Not so, networking is about genuine, sincere exchanges.

4. **Great networkers are all extroverts.**
   Connections and relationships are developed through learning. Networkers are made, not born.

5. **Networking takes too much time.**
   It does take time but schedule it in each week and make it a part of your marketing plan. Do you have the time not to? Referrals and word of mouth will make up 70% or higher of your business.

6. **I built my network, it will always be there.**
   All relationships require care and nurturing. Without continual maintenance, networks will eventually die off.

7. **I'll look like a failure if I ask for help.**
   Not true. You look like an individual who is growing a business. Most people will enjoy helping you especially when they see potential for reciprocity in the future.

8. **I offer superior service: I don't need connections and my work speaks for itself.**
   How many people actually know your work? With a networking circle you can grow your business more efficiently and effectively.

9. **I can't possibly meet the right people.**
   Who really are the right people? It is amazing the people that you can meet through networking.

10. **I can't network virtually.**
    Of course you can, and you must. Developing your virtual network and building on line communities is imperative for your business success.

Different Types of Networking Groups

There are a variety of different networking groups. Here are a few just to give you some ideas:

Industry Groups: These groups are dedicated to specific industries. As a Virtual Assistant, you will find that these groups are growing rapidly. The majority of these networking group are very supportive and a wonderful way to meet your virtual colleagues. Industry groups are great for keeping up on the latest information and industry news. Keep in mind that networking with other Virtual Assistants is a great way to also build your referrals and be a resource for other VA's who may have a full practice.

Local Business Groups: There are numerous small business groups within your area. Your local chamber of commerce or business to business networking groups are a great way to dip your foot in the networking pool. Local business groups not only provide a wonderful way to build your referral network but also provide a great way to get involved within your community.

Service-oriented groups: Groups such as Rotary, Lions and others support worthy causes and provide a social setting for networking.

Virtual groups: There are an increasing number of "virtual" groups available online, apart from the VA organizations. There are interest groups, forums and discussion groups that you can choose.

"Free time" groups: The best way to network is when you are doing it while having fun. Free time groups mean the country club, baseball games, art class, etc. Add an activity to your life, it is the best way to meet new friends and friends are the best source for referrals.

Trade shows: Being an exhibitor at a trade show is an excellent place to network and introduce your business to the participants. However, even if you want to attend a trade show as a participant as opposed to being an exhibitor – there are plenty of opportunities for networking.

Tips for exhibiting at a trade show

You will have many opportunities to take a booth or table top to exhibit your services. Here are a few tips for an effective display:

- If you plan on exhibiting a lot, invest in a table top display, the most cost effective booth. It will provide you with a professional look and not break the bank. The cost for a table top display runs approximately $500 to $1,000, but worth the investment.

- Let your existing clients and prospective clients know you will be exhibiting at the event. Invite them to come see you.

- Create a friendly atmosphere. Introduce yourself to exhibitors on either side of you. Greet people as they come by your table.

- Have an attention-getting sign and incorporate your benefits into the information.

- Provide handouts or tips that people will keep because the information is valuable.

- Do not overwhelm visitors by too much information. Instead of bringing all your information, have a sign up sheet so you can send them more information after the show.

- If within budget, provide free give always, such as a book mark, pen, pencils, etc. Make sure you have your company name and contact information on each item.

- Offer a free subscription to your newsletter or have a draw for complimentary services.

Your Thirty Second Elevator Pitch

Imagine getting into an elevator in an office building. As the doors close, the person next to you says, "A colleague of mine said you are a Virtual Assistant; what do you do?"

You have exactly thirty seconds or less before the elevator reaches the bottom floor to effectively tell this person what you do.

The thirty second elevator pitch is something you need to practice and perfect. It is a basic introduction of who you are, what you do, who you do it for and what the benefit is to the person who hires you. It will form the basis of your introductory message when networking and when a new client contacts you.

As you reach out to network with others, you will be required to cut to the chase quickly. Most contacts want a clear, direct approach and are not looking for your life history. It is important for you to develop a level of comfort in your personal presentation and you can achieve this by practicing the delivery of your Thirty Second Elevator Pitch as much as you can.

Creating your Elevator Pitch

Here is an easy to use formula that will help you create your elevator pitch:

1. My name is _____.

2. I am a _____ who assists _____(who, what type of people do you assist) by _____ (what is it that you assist them with) so they _____ (what are the benefits).

You can be more elaborate by including answers to other questions such as:

- What is the advantage of hiring you over someone else?
- Why are you unique?
- How do you assist people (virtually, in person)?
- What is your niche?

Here are a few samples to help you along:

I'm Jane Smith. I'm a Virtual Assistant who assists Real Estate agents virtually from home by using the Internet and email; I manage their client contacts and prospective clients allowing them more time to follow up on leads.

Hi I'm Amanda Jones, a Virtual Assistant. I support small businesses with their administrative tasks from bookkeeping to document preparation. I do this from my home office so my clients do not need to worry about finding space for me.

Hi my name is Mary Black. As a Virtual Assistant, I provide administrative support to clients worldwide. By utilizing today's technology such as the Internet and email, I am able to provide professional administrative support to any business. This enables my clients to focus on running their business, instead of their business running them.

All of these samples are simple, direct and will peak their interest, so they will want to know more.

Delivering your Elevator Pitch

You must deliver your pitch with confidence and passion. Speak clearly, smoothly and slower than usual. Practice your pitch in the mirror if you feel this will help or ask a friend or family member to listen and ask for feedback. Do it over and over again until you can do it in your sleep.

You never know what opportunity will cross your path, so be prepared.

Building Community

Being a part of a community, whether it is a person-to-person community or a virtual community, is really the "heart" of being a Virtual Assistant. It is what is unique about this profession. Building community is an important part of not only being a Virtual Assistant but in the success of your practice.

There are many on-line associations and organizations that promote the idea of developing community within the VA profession. These associations and organizations can be wonderful resources when promoting your business.

In most cases these associations/organizations offer membership at a nominal fee. For this membership fee you will have access to on-line materials, a listing in their directory and be a part of a community.

Some of these associations/organizations will also host networking calls, in person networking events and opportunities for you to meet your fellow VA's.

There are plenty of benefits for joining on-line organizations such as:

- Meet others in the same profession
- Helps to deal with the isolation of working from home
- Submit requests for proposal (If a client comes to the site and requests a work proposal, as a member you will be able to submit one)
- Inclusion in their directory
- No geographical boundaries
- Networking opportunities
- Volunteer opportunities
- Referral opportunities
- Industry tips and information

Like with everything you invest your money in, make sure that it is right for you. Not all organizations promote the profession; some are just out to make a few dollars. Before you join any organization, consider these suggestions:

- Research the organization as much as possible.
- Speak with other members and ask them how they like the organization.
- Read their code of ethics and any membership agreements before joining.
- Ask yourself what you want to get out of joining a particular organization.

Benefits of Community:

1. **Relationship-building**
   Building relationships is what marketing is all about. By being a part of a community you are building much needed relationships to grow your business.

2. **Referral generation**
   By being a part of a community, you are opening yourself up to possibilities of referrals from colleagues. If you build those relationships and build the trust within your community, others will be comfortable referring your services.

3. **Wealth of information**
   You will have a wealth of information right at your finger tips – use it.

4. **Become a leader**
   By being an active participant in your community, you will gain the respect and trust of others in the community. Let your voice be heard, become a leader.

5. **Helps with isolation**
   At times you feel very isolated from the rest of the world, sitting alone in your home office. By being part of a community, you are surrounded by others who deal with the same issues and experiences. Extend yourself to your community.

With the advent of computer networks and "virtual communities", however, some feel that electronic technologies can actually be used to strengthen the bonds of community and reverse America's declining social capital. Advocates stress that electronic networks can help citizens build organizations, provide local information, and develop bonds of civic life and conviviality. While the claims are no doubt overstated in many cases, as they always are when new technologies are involved, there is growing evidence that this may be the case, particularly in local community networks.

Robert Putnam
The Strange Disappearance of Civic America

Chapter 10 - Summary

Networking is really about relationships. It is about building friendships with people who we would also like to do business with...it is a simple as that!

Referrals and Word of Mouth

Throughout this book, we frequently mention the importance of referrals and word of mouth. As a Virtual Assistant, you will find that the majority of your business will come from both of these.

Referring back to Chapter One – Introduction to Marketing and the marketing cycle, you see that by building successful working relationships with clients, it leads to the development and attainment of those necessary referrals to build your business.

Virtual Assistance is not unlike any other service-based profession in the sense that if you have happy, satisfied clients, you will receive repeat business as well as new business that they have referred to you.

The diagram to the right shows how simple it really is.

Word of mouth and referrals are all about providing the best quality of service possible.

By providing the best possible service, your clients are satisfied and you have began the steps to building a solid working relationship and have obtained their confidence.

Once they trust your service they will feel comfortable in giving your name to others they come in contact.

This is all common sense.

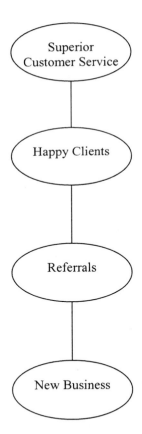

Referrals do not necessarily need to come from just your clients or for people that you have done work. Referrals can come from a variety of sources: people you have met at networking events, resources that you have used in your business, or even friends and family.

The most common reason people give referrals is because they like you or your service. If you are new in business, you will need to start with referrals from non-clients who know you in other ways. As discussed in Chapter Ten – Networking, you need to talk and tell everyone what you are doing and that you are looking for business.

Building Confidence

Everything you do for a client will help to build confidence, providing you are doing the right things, even small simple actions can be powerful.

A few are listed below:

Provide realistic time lines and meet them
Never over-promise. Always be realistic when determining the length of time for a project and always meet those timelines. Clients who expect their work completed within a certain time frame will be very disappointed when this is not met and will quickly lose confidence in your ability to provide work in a timely manner.

Be solution oriented
The best way to build client confidence is to be there for a client when they have a problem and provide a solution to help them through it. You should approach all client relationships as a partnership and view your client's problem as your problem, and find a solution.

Be courteous
Being friendly and courteous really does go a long way.

Go above and beyond the call of duty
Take your work a step further. Do something for your client that they did not ask for or expect to have done. This could be as simple as sending an article to your client that you feel would be of interest to them.

Provide resources
If you cannot help them, have a list of resources that you can give them. Make sure these resources have proven track records.

Always communicate the truth
Your clients will not think any less of you if you are unsure of a project or do not have the skills to do it. Be truthful with them and they will appreciate your honesty.

Only provide services you do well

Do not add items to your service list for the sake of having a larger service list. Only add those services that you do very well. If you know a little bit about bookkeeping – not good enough. You need to know a lot about bookkeeping in order to offer this as a viable service.

Building Relationships

There are a variety of ways that you can build relationships, so much so that it actually becomes second nature to us, we do not consciously realize we are doing it.

When trying to develop a business through relationship building, word of mouth and referrals, you will have to try to be aware of your relationship building technique.

A few things to always consider:

Be a friend

Not only provide services to your clients but offer your friendship as well. When we talk about friendship, we do not mean you have to begin spending your weekends at their house, or go on shopping trips together. Form a relationship that is comfortable to you. People love to talk about their interests outside of work, so listen and spark up conversation regarding this - be personable.

> "So, how was your trip to the cottage this weekend?"
> "How was your son's birthday party?"
> "You sound tired, is everything okay?"

These are simple questions that show your client that you listen and have a genuine interest in their life outside of work.

Be giving

Everyone loves to receive something at one time or another. We do not mean buying your client's affections; we are talking about offering a gesture of gratitude. This can be as simple as buying a thank you card, thanking your client for their business.

Share

Share your experiences, share your thoughts, and share your resources and connections. Share anything with a client that you feel will help to build a relationship.

Talk about yourself
A majority of clients will love to hear about you, your family, and your business anything that helps them get a clearer understanding of the person who is doing their work. Remember to be appropriate when divulging information about yourself. There are some things you should talk about and other things left unsaid.

Types of Referrals

Client Referrals
These are the referrals you get by providing great customer service and the most rewarding type of referral.

Professional Referrals
Referrals you receive from other Virtual Assistants, these referrals are generated through on-going networking and relationship building within the profession.

Resource Referrals
These types of referrals are from resources you use within your business. Web designers, printers, accountants and bookkeepers often make fantastic referral sources. If possible, create alliances with other professions and provide reciprocal referrals: win–win for everyone.

Association Referrals
Some associations will provide your name as a referral if you meet the criteria of a prospective client. These types of referrals are not too common and keep in mind that most associations are required to give the name of at least three other businesses when giving referrals.

Asking for Referrals

Asking for referrals may not be easy for some people, however, you need to get over it. As a VA, referrals are your lifeblood.

To help you gain confidence in this area, here are a few things to know about asking for referrals.

- Ask for referrals outright. Explain what you do and would appreciate referrals. It is as simple as that. Of course, you are not going to ask a complete stranger who knows nothing about you to refer clients to you. You are going to build relationships or use existing relationships with people to build your referral base.

- Build your reputation. This takes time by providing exceptional client service. When you are good at what you do and have confidence in your ability, asking for referrals will become second nature.

- Be involved in an atmosphere where referrals can occur. People refer people who they like and trust. This means you need to get out and talk with confidence about what it is you do and about the clients you work with. As covered in the previous chapter, networking is an important part in getting the word out. Join your local chamber of commerce, go to seminars or join a health club. Even social activities can provide great opportunities for networking.

- Do not come from a place of desperation. If you are desperate for clients and are needy, people will sense this and run the other way. Think of it this way: if you were to walk into a bank and say, "I am desperate, I need money." That is a reason why you want the money; it is not a reason why the bank should give it to you. The same applies for referrals.

- Be clear on the terms of the referral. Some people will give you referrals just because they like you and want to help you. Others may see something in it for themselves. Be sure that there is not a hidden agenda when someone refers business to you.

- Give referrals to get referrals. When you provide a referral for another business that you trust explicitly and you know they will provide the best service possible, this will reflect on you. Best-case scenario: the happy customer will then send business your way.

- Offer referral fees or free services. Let everyone know that if they refer someone to you, they will receive a referral fee or, preferably, two or three hours of free services.

- Thank those who refer you. Once someone refers you, the relationship does not stop there. Send them a thank you note or a small gift. Keep in contact with them and remind them of how appreciative you are for the referrals.

Word of Mouth

"Word of mouth is far and away the dominant force in the marketplace. Yet it is also the most neglected. Companies have vice presidents of sales, advertising and marketing. Yet there isn't a single vice president of word of mouth in any corporation in the country. Why?"

- *George Silverman, Author*

An amusing quote, yet so true. Spreading the word on your business and the services you offer is just as important as those necessary referrals. You have to build your reputation and your credibility as a Virtual Assistant who provides superior client service.

Sometimes spreading the word is not as easy as it sounds. People need to witness and experience the results themselves in order to confidently spread the word.

For these individuals, let them do just that. Offer a free hour of services or a complimentary intake session to discuss their administrative challenges and the solutions you can provide for them. You will find that they will be intrigued to take you up on your offer.

The great thing about being a VA is the "newness" of the profession. The term Virtual Assistant itself will peak interest and start conversation. Not only between you and the person you are speaking to, but guaranteed the next day that same person will be telling someone else about this new profession they heard about called Virtual Assisting. And of course your name will come up.

Every time you talk about what it is you do, you are creating a chain effect. This is the very basis of word of mouth. So, you can see the importance of talking and talking a lot about your business.

> I met a woman the other day who is a Virtual Assistant.

> Really. A Virtual Assistant? What does a Virtual Assistant do?

The conversation starts and word of mouth begins.

10 Quick Tips for Generating Word of Mouth Referrals

1. As mentioned earlier…ask for them.

2. Be specific. Provide people with a few details about your target market.

3. Develop word of mouth marketing promotions. Develop a marketing plan that encourages referrals.

4. Promote positive feedback. Ask clients to evaluate your services and provide feedback on the service they are receiving.

5. Encourage self-development. Make a commitment to life long learning. Constantly grow and develop your knowledge.

6. Build a customer community. Find way to bring your clients together. This may include teleconferencing, chat rooms or inviting clients to an event.

7. Leverage your competitive advantage. In your promotional activities, feature what sets your business apart from the competition in the eyes of your clients.

8. Become an excellent listener. Communication skills are extremely important in trust building with clients.

9. Enjoy networking. Establish a networking plan built around helping others.

10. Develop an eye-catching website. When web surfers come across an interesting site, it is not uncommon for them to tell others about it.

Start getting referrals NOW!

How will you make yourself a topic of conversation for your clients? List ten good reasons that your clients might talk about you; these questions may help:

- What is unique about your service?
- Why is it so valuable to your clients that they know and trust you?
- What is new that you do that not many people know about?
- What good feedback have your clients recently given you, and how could you do more of what they find valuable?

When people talk about you more, you will notice the difference:

- You will spend more time SERVING people and less energy selling to them.
- You will be able to spend more time doing the things you like to do as opposed to marketing your business.
- You will be more confident and find it easier to talk with people about what you do.

Word of Mouth Worksheet

Place an X in the appropriate yes or no column.

YES	NO	QUESTIONS
		I send referrals to my clients.
		My clients, friends and professional network know who I like to work with.
		I update my network regularly as I change specialty / upgrade my service through training, etc.
		I have a newsletter that is easy to run and gives value for people.
		I help people to experience what I do rather than telling them about it.
		My clients have all my details and spare business cards to give to others.
		I thank people for referrals.
		I know the eight people who send me the most business, and I have a strong relationship with them.
		I continually improve my product/service and have an easy system for informing my circle.
		When a client is dissatisfied, I take three 'over the top' actions to make sure it will never happen again.

You should have an X under the YES column for each question. Start by doing these items as a regular routine and set up reminders for each of these procedures.

Chapter 11 - Summary

Throughout this book we have covered a variety of marketing techniques that could be the basis for all your marketing. However, referrals and word of mouth are the most effective, least expensive marketing methods for obtaining new clients.

You should also be aware that referrals do not just happen; you need to cultivate and build relationships.

Creating your Marketing Plan

Goals in writing are dreams with deadlines.
-Brian Tracy

Just as you have discovered if you have ever written a business plan, there are many variations in the format and outlines for marketing plans. It is up to you and only you to decide how extensive you want your marketing plan to be.

You need to decide the purpose of your marketing plan. If you will be using your marketing plan to attain a loan for business start up at a financial institution, you will be required to provide a very detailed and extensive plan. If your marketing plan is only for your benefit, to help you get clearer on your marketing initiatives and goals, it can be simpler and less formal.

We will be looking at two different variations:

1) A simple, mini marketing plan
2) A more extensive overall marketing plan

Keep in mind, even if you start with the simpler plan of the two, it can be revised and added to when you have a need to do so. The simpler plan will give you a good basis for the more extensive marketing plan.

As a VA in a sole practice, you may find that you do not necessarily need a more extensive plan, and you would be in the majority. It is not too often that a VA will find use for a more extensive and highly detailed marketing plan. However, if the urge to expand your marketing initiatives grabs you then we applaud your efforts and encourage you to take a look at the extensive marketing plan within this chapter.

Benefits of Planning

- A plan will encourage you to do research
- A plan will help you learn more about yourself and your business initiatives
- A plan helps you direct your efforts to get you where you want to be
- A plan will motivate you to reach your specific goals
- A plan will help you organize your ideas
- A plan will give you clear timelines to reach your goals

Planning requires some guesswork.

If you are at the beginning stages of starting your business, you will find that you will be required to do quite a bit of guesswork when working on your marketing plan. Forecasting will be required, but do not let it discourage you, be realistic when goal setting and setting your budget and you will do just fine. Remember, some amazing things have been accomplished by guesswork.

So let's begin!!

Getting Started

Up to this point you should have all or most of the information you need to begin creating your marketing plan. To help you start planning, it is easier to have all your information in one place. To refresh your memory on topics we have covered in previous chapters, use the Marketing worksheet below:

Marketing Worksheet

Business Name _____

Services you plan to offer

_____
_____
_____

Our service will sell because:

_____
_____
_____
_____

Describe the benefits your service will offer customers (the SPECIFIC problems the service solves or SPECIFIC advantages it offers to the customer)

_____
_____
_____
_____
_____
_____

Location and Type of Market

Our market will be:

❑ Local   ❑ International   ❑ National   ❑ Province or State Wide

❑ Combination   ❑ Other

Our typical client is:

❑ An individual   ❑ A family   ❑ A business   ❑ Government

The typical client is located in:

❑ Rural area   ❑ Suburbs   ❑ Large city

Typical Individual Client

The customer is:

❑ Male   ❑ Female   ❑ Male or Female

The typical client's income level is:

❑ $50,000 or less   ❑ $50,000 - $70,000   ❑ $70,000 - $100,000   ❑ No typical level

The typical client will require:

❑ All services   ❑ 4-5 Services   ❑ 1-3 Services   ❑ No typical level

The majority of services needed are:

❑ Daily Basis   ❑ Weekly Basis   ❑ Monthly Basis   ❑ No typical level

The principal reason a client will pay for our services is:

_____

_____

_____

_____

_____

The number of clients in our market is:

❑ Increasing   ❑ Constant   ❑ Decreasing

Competition

How many other services like yours are in your area?

_____

How will your service differ from your competitors?

_____
_____
_____
_____
_____
_____

Is there any particular industry jargon, knowledge or past work experience you possess that would give you an edge over competitors if you focused on bringing in business from a particular industry? (Example: have you ever worked in a law office, typed statistical data, etc.)

_____

Getting Clients

How are you planning to find clients? (Check all that apply)

_____Mailings
_____In-person sales calls
_____Phone calls
_____Paid advertising in newspapers or magazines
_____Classified ads
_____Ads on the Internet
_____An ad in the Yellow pages
_____Word-of-mouth advertising
_____Network at business meetings
_____Window signs to attract walk-in trade
_____In-store displays to sell add-on services
_____Bidding on jobs
_____Online classified advertising or websites
_____Other (specify)

Our target audience for advertising is:

_____

The geographic area for our advertising will be:

_____

Our advertising budget will be:

$ _____ in the 1st year
$ _____ in the 2nd year
$ _____ in the 3rd year

What will it cost you to use each of these marketing methods?

_____Mailings (Include cost of postage, mailing lists, if they will be rented, and printed
       materials. If you will create the mailers on your own printer, be sure to include
       the cost of paper and ink.)
_____In-person sales calls (include gas money)
_____Phone calls
_____Paid advertising
_____Classified ads
_____Small display ads
_____Yellow pages
_____Word-of-mouth advertising
_____Network at business meetings (include cost of meetings, if any)
_____Banner ads on the Internet
_____Ads in electronic newsletters
_____Bidding on jobs
_____Online classified advertising or websites
_____Other (specify)

We will evaluate our marketing effectiveness by:

_____
_____
_____

Once you have answered these questions you will have the basis to start on your marketing plan.

A Mini Marketing Plan (MMP) in Four Easy Steps

A mini marketing plan is the simplest way to begin planning and implementing your marketing efforts. As stated earlier in this chapter, this type of marketing plan would not be detailed enough for a business start up loan; it is a great way to clarify your personal planning purpose, marketing goals and initiatives.

1) What are your goals of marketing?

Goal #1: _____

It is important to keep this answer simple, direct and specific. Making more money or getting more clients is too general.

Here are some more specific examples:

- To get (state number) *new* clients within the Real Estate Profession
- To get publicity in the "Franklin City Times"
- To get repeat clients
- To get (state number) referrals from each client

These goals may even be more specific such as to get on a local radio show or to become a guest writer in a trade magazine or newspaper. Choose a goal that is realistic and achievable.

2) What are the action items to reach your goals?

Goal #1 _____

Action: _____

Action Items are the steps you will be taking to help you reach your goals. The action items may be as simple as making a telephone call.

Goal 1: Increase awareness of VA's R US within the business community.

Actions:
- Attend at least four networking events every three months
- Advertise in at least three mediums per year
- Join two networking organizations a year
- Donate services to local charities

Goal 2: Get new clients within the Real Estate profession

Actions:
- Create a database of Real Estate professionals
- Create a hard copy mailing introducing my services
- Offer a discount on services if contacted within a certain timeline
- Follow up by telephone to at least 20% of the people that received the direct mailing

3) What is your marketing budget?

I will spend _____ hours per week on marketing.

I have _____ dollars to spend.

Each year I would like to increase my marketing budget by _____.

As a small business, you will need to budget enough time and money to get results. If you currently have no clients, you should be marketing most of the time.

4) What is your schedule for action?

Tomorrow I will _____
_____
_____

Tomorrow I will work _____ hours.

I have scheduled these days and times during the week to work on marketing.

Day   Time
_____   _____
_____   _____
_____   _____
_____   _____
_____   _____

By the end of this week, I will have accomplished _____
_____
_____
_____

By the end of the month, I will have worked a total of _____ hours on marketing.

At the end of the month, I will have accomplished _____
_____
_____
_____
_____
_____

By committing to a specific schedule, it is easier to motivate yourself to reach your goals. A schedule is a direct commitment for taking action on a particular action at a particular time. It helps you to focus to finish your mini marketing plan.

Important to Note:

With the simplicity of this mini marketing plan, it is still imperative that you understand who is your target audience, what is your niche, what your company identity says about you and who are your competitors. Although this mini plan does not discuss all these items, you should still be clear on all of these points.

The Extensive Marketing Plan (EMP)

The best place to start with this marketing plan is at the beginning, with an understanding of what you hope to accomplish in your business and a feel for the strategies that will best help you to achieve those goals.

As mentioned earlier, this type of plan is a fairly extensive plan and will require you to think and look ahead. It will also require you to do a fair bit of research and approach this research with an analytical mind.

History has shown that there is one reason why some people succeed and others fail. The difference is not one of knowing, but of doing. It is not so much of what you know but the actions in which you take.

EMP Overview

Typically your EMP should include the following sections:

1. Executive Summary
2. Market Review
3. Competitive Analysis
4. Product/Service Review
5. Strength, Weaknesses, Opportunities, Threats (SWOT)
6. Goals and Objectives
7. Strategies
8. Action Plan and Implementation
9. Evaluation

Executive Summary

The Executive Summary is usually the first section of a marketing plan. It summarizes your plan for quick review and is normally written last. Once you have completed the meat of your plan, come back and write your executive summary.

The Executive Summary should briefly cover:

1. Market Review
2. Competitive Review
3. Product/Service Review
4. Strength, Weaknesses, Opportunities, Threats (SWOT)
5. Goals and Objectives
6. Strategies
7. Action Plan and Implementation
8. Evaluation

The executive summary could be from a paragraph to a couple of pages long. Outside readers may only read this and then glance to one or two sections.

Market Review

For this section of your marketing plan you will need to do a bit of research and find the answers for the following questions:

1. Who are the major users of your services (be as specific as possible)?
2. How big is the potential market?
3. Is the market growing, at a stand still or decreasing? What changes do you see happening?
4. Is the market segmented by location, quality, age, income or services?
5. Who is your target audience?
6. Who are your competitors?

As with all of the other sections of your marketing plan, there is no right or wrong way to organize your information. Organize the market overview section in a way that makes sense to you.

Target Market

In this section or your marketing plan, go into as much detail as possible about who is your market. Include items such as:

- Age
- Sex
- Profession
- Income level
- Educational level

Find out as much as possible about your target market.

Example:

At VA's R US, our target market consists of Personal and Business Coaches who primarily work from their home offices. The majority of this market is women from the ages of 39-45 and have a post-secondary education and have formally been trained as a Personal and Business Coach by a training institute that specializes in this type of training.

Our target market consists of Coaches who have an annual income of $60,000 to $100,000. These Coaches are more apt to have the financial resources to hire a Virtual Assistant.

Here are some other questions you may want to answer and include in the Market Review section of your marketing plan.

1. What do clients like about your services?
2. What do they like about your competitors' services?
3. What made them decide to hire you?
4. What advertising message have they seen prior to hiring you, if any?
5. What emotional aspects impact their purchase?
6. Who is the decision-maker for this type of hiring?
7. What values and attitudes played a part in this hire?

Competitive Analysis

For this section of your marketing plan, you will want to provide a complete and thorough overview of your competitive market. Cover not only those companies you are directly competing with (companies that offer the same service, same profession), but also other companies outside of the profession. For example: As a VA you are not only competing with other VA's you are also competing against temporary placement agencies that provide administrative professionals to companies on a temporary basis.

Describe your competitors and answer the following questions:

1. What are their strengths and weaknesses as a company?
2. What are the differences between your services and theirs?
3. What is their pricing structure?
4. What were their sales last year?
5. In what media mediums do they advertise their services?
6. What is their advertising message?
7. Where else do they promote their services?
8. What were their total advertising expenditures for last year?
9. What is their overall goal?
10. How are they trying to meet their goals (low prices, better quality)?

Information is often the key to a strong competitive advantage. Visit your competitors' websites, request information or even just ask them the questions.

Product/Service Review

Use this section of your marketing plan to fully describe:

- Your service and its purpose
- Its features

- Current pricing structure
- Delivery your services
- Current promotions and advertising

Make sure the information is specific and accurate. This part of your marketing plan should be easy for you. You know the services you are offering; you should also know what benefits your clients will receive from your services.

In a nutshell, you have to make the end result very clear that is ultimately the reason why someone should hire you.

SWOT Analysis

SWOT stands for strengths, weaknesses, opportunities and threats. Strengths and weaknesses are internal factors. For example, a strength could be your expertise with web design. A weakness could be the lack of a service such as bookkeeping.

Opportunities and threats are external factors. An opportunity could be the development of new software that could be used on a developing market. A threat could be a new competitor in your target market.

**A word of caution: SWOT analysis can be very subjective. Because it is based on people's perceptions rather than hard data, take the results with a grain of salt.

SWOT begins by looking at internal strengths and weaknesses. To help you determine these, use the chart:

Factors	Strength	Weakness
Profitability		
Sales and Marketing		
Quality		
Customer Service		
Productivity		
Financial Resources		
Financial Management		
Operations		

Internal strengths and weaknesses are easy. For each key area, ask yourself whether it is a strength or a weakness – it may be both. You are looking for a rough profile of your business's internal performance. You want to be able to capitalize on the strengths and defend or improve weaknesses.

Now you will need to look at the external environments where your business operates. While these factors are not under your control, if you examine how they will affect you, you can take precautionary action.

Factors	Opportunities	Threats
Current Clients		
Prospective Clients		
Competition		
Technology		
Government		
Economic environment		

Again for each factor, ask what opportunities and threats to the success for your business are coming up.

Technological factors include new or improved technologies. For example, desktop publishing software is becoming easier and friendlier to use – is this an opportunity, threat or both??

Government factors could include taxes for small businesses, regulations and new laws for doing business outside of the country.

Economic environments – local, national and international – will have a direct impact on your business. For example, if you charge your clients in US dollars and the US dollar plummets, this can directly affect your financial goals. However, if the US dollar rises significantly, it will have a positive affect on your financial position. Threat or opportunity?

Once you have completed both charts, pick five strengths and opportunities to work on and no more than five weaknesses and threats.

SWOT Summary

The most important strengths we possess and the best opportunities we face are:
1)
2)
3)
4)
5)

The most dangerous weaknesses and threats we face are:
1)
2)
3)
4)
5)

Now create your action list to build on your strengths and opportunities and to improve your weaknesses and threats.

Examples:

#1 Strength or Opportunity:	Excellent reputation
Action:	Leverage word of mouth, ask for referrals

#1 Weakness or Threat:	New competitors
Action:	Provide more personal service, build solid relationships with existing clients, fast response times

Your SWOT analysis is now complete. Include all your charts and your action list in your marketing plan.

Goals and Objectives

Without goals we would never get anywhere or do anything in life. As described in the Mini Marketing plan with Goals and Actions, the same concept applies here within the Goals and Objectives section of your marketing plan.

There is a distinction between goals and objectives. Goals are long-range, anywhere from a year to many years and help you maintain your business direction. Objectives are short-range, specific activities that are tactics to move you towards your long-term goals.

You need two sets of goals: One for your business and one for yourself. Personal goals come first.

To set your personal goals ask yourself these questions (you may have already answered some of these questions if you completed the marketing worksheet at the beginning of this chapter):

1. How much money do you want or need to earn?
2. What sort of lifestyle is desirable for you and your family?
3. How big do you want your business to become?
4. How will your business reflect you and your values?
5. How much risk do you want to take? In what areas?
6. What do you want to achieve over the next five years?

Now that you have a clearer understanding of what your personal goals are you will be able to create business goals that are aligned with your personal desires.

Sales and Marketing Goals

After completing your personal goals, now focus on your business goals and more specifically your sales goals and marketing objectives. Start with your sales goals first.

For each service that you offer, forecast sales for the next year. A worst case/best case/most likely case approach makes this somewhat easier and more accurate than just guessing. Use the chart below; some services have already been filled out, complete according to your offered services.

Services	Worst Case	Most Likely Case	Best Case
Word Processing			
Bookkeeping			
Desktop Publishing			
Web Design			
Database Management			
EX:			
Word Processing	$500.00/year	$1500.00/year	$3000.00/year

For each service, estimate what sales would be if everything goes wrong next year. Then estimate what sales would be if everything goes perfectly. Since neither case is likely, indicate the most likely case scenario. This number is not an average of worst and best cases, but rather your opinion of what will happen to each service over the next year.

For the example, keep in mind as a VA you will have ongoing clients that will require word processing on a regular basis and other clients who are more project-to-project. It is a good idea to estimate your sales per service. You may have a client who requires bookkeeping, word processing and web design; try to forecast these figures individually as opposed to combining them.

By forecasting these services separately, it will also give you an indication which services you predict will be the real money makers.

Marketing Objectives

Your marketing objectives should be the means to achieve your sales goals. Some marketing objectives could be increased sales, improved market share, entry into new markets or adding a new service. Your objectives could even include improving your company image, advertising or promotional efforts.

Marketing Objectives Examples:

1) Create a website that clearly defines benefits of services for promotion.
2) Create a 5,000-person database of potential clients for distribution of marketing material.
3) Add two new services this year.

Set Goals for the future. Although your marketing plan need only to forecast for the next year, try forecasting your sales goals for the next three years to provide direction, stability and help you to maintain your focus.

**For next year, add "most likely case" figures.

Services	For next year	In three years
Word Processing		
Bookkeeping		
Desktop Publishing		
Web Design		
Database management		
EX:		
*Word Processing *￼*	$1,500.00	$3,500.00

* This sample shows that we have forecasted our Increase in sales to be $1,000 per year.

Strategies

The strategies portion of your marketing plan will need to cover the following:

Service/Product Strategy

Your service strategy is the nuts and bolts of your service list and why someone would hire you to perform them. Discuss the features and benefits of your services and what makes you different from your competitors.

Pricing Strategy

This discusses how you will be pricing your services. Are your prices too low or too high or competitive within the industry?

Some things to think about:

1) Although your strategy may be to offer lower prices than your competitors, consider the reflection this may have on your services. Does this communicate that your services are inferior to your competitors?
2) Will pricing your services at the higher end of the scale hurt your chances of getting clients or will it communicate that your service is supreme?

When writing your pricing strategies, back it up with current data about your competitors' prices.

Promotion Strategy

Your promotion strategy is the section of your marketing plan where you will discuss the tools you will use to promote yourself.

This section should cover the following items:

- Advertising
- Relationship building (word of mouth, referrals)
- Direct marketing
- Promotions and events
- Marketing materials
- Other promotions

You will discuss the action plan and implementation of these items in the next section.

Action and Implementation

This section of your marketing plan is where you put words into action. You will want to show the reader how you plan to implement your strategy more specifically your promotional strategies.

To help you better organize this consider using a chart as shown below:

Promotional Strategy	Action	Cost	Deadline
Advertising	Place ad in 'Franklin Times'	$250.00	Jan 4/04
	Place pay per click banner ad on Real Estate resource site	$100.00 - $300.00	Mar 30/04
Direct Mailing	Create 2000 person database	$0.00	Apr 10/04
	Create flyer for mailings	$30.00	Apr 12/04
	Buy stamps for mailings	$102.00	Apr 13/04
	Complete mail out	$0.00	Apr 15/04

Be as detailed as possible when listing your actions and as realistic as possible when listing your deadlines.

Evaluation

For the last section of your marketing plan, you will need to include information on how you plan on tracking your successes and losses for each promotional marketing strategy you are using – how you will be determining what works and what does not.

This could be as simple as asking prospective clients how they heard about you or tracking the number of enquires you receive after an ad is placed.

Chapter 12 - Summary

Your marketing initiatives do not stop after you have created your marketing plan. Review your plan quarterly. Ask yourself where your business is coming from, existing clients or new clients? What is your competition doing? What is your overall position in the market?

Your plan will be an evolutionary process; from year to year you will find new and improved ways to market your business and will be able to add these initiatives to your existing marketing plan.

Keep up the planning, goal setting and implementation!

CONCLUSION

As the pages of this book come to an end, I want to reiterate the meaning behind this guide and the VA approach to marketing.

The VA approach to marketing is about:

- Not just building sales, but building relationships.
- Doing all that's in your power to provide the most sincere, unmatched form of superior client service.
- Providing and offering only those services that you do well and with integrity.
- Understanding the importance of finding YOUR ideal client.
- Creating community

And above all else…LOVING what it is you are doing. If you're not doing something that you love and are passionate about then no means of marketing will make your practice a success.

Good Luck and Best Wishes

M. Jamison

GLOSSARY OF TERMS

Advertising - Advertising is bringing a service to the attention of potential current customers. Advertising is done with items such as signs, brochures, mailings, etc.

Branding - is a name, terms, design, symbol, feature and/or identity which distinguishes your service or services, from others.

Client Information Package – A marketing tool that you send to prospective clients that contains important information about you, your company and your services. It can be in hard copy or e-version.

Company Identity – are the various characteristics by which you and your service are recognized and known.

Company Image - is how your business identity is perceived by customers, professional associated, the media, and the public at large.

Core Values - outline the ethics and values of the organization, creating a pledge to its staff, clients and the world at large.

Logo - a name, symbols or trademark designed for easy recognition.

Marketing - Marketing is anything you do to get or keep a customer. Marketing is a wide range of activities involved in making sure that you are continuing to meet the needs of your customers and getting value in return.

Marketing Kit – A term to describe your marketing materials all of your marketing materials. It is an imaginary marketing treasure chest that contains all of your company marketing material.

Mission statement- is a short written description of the aims of a business, charity, government department or public organization. "

Niche - Similar to target marketing, however more specific.

Promotion - Promotion keeps the service in the minds of the customer and helps stimulate demand for the services. Promotion involves ongoing advertising and publicity.

Publicity - Publicity is mention in the medial. With publicity you usually have little control over the message in the media, far less than with advertising.

Public Relations - Public relations includes ongoing activities to ensure the company has a strong public image.

Rifle Marketing - You are clear on whom it is you are aiming your marketing message at. You have a particular type of client to whom you are marketing your services.

Sales - Sales involves selling your service to potential clients. It allows for the personal touch.

Shotgun Marketing - You are spraying your message all over the place hoping that some of it will hit. You are unclear of the type of client would use your services so you bombard everyone with your marketing message.

Tagline - is used to better explain what your business does and to create an impression about your company and/or service.

Target Market - Those individuals to whom you target your services.

Vision - the ability to imagine how a country, society, industry, etc. will develop in the future and to plan in a suitable way"

Website Terminology

Domain name - A name that identifies one or more IP addresses. Domain names are used in URLs to identify particular Web Pages that make up a Web Site.

> **TLD** - Top Level Domain – refers to .com. net .org

> **CcTLD** - Country Code Top Level Domains – refers to .ca – Canada, .au – Australia

Keywords - (Meta Tag) A group of words describing the content of a web page used by search engines to index the Web site

Meta tags – A special HTML tag that provides information about a Web page but does not change the way the page is displayed.

Search engines – A program that searches documents for specified keywords and returns a list of the documents where the keywords were found.

Site navigation – The links on a website that help you navigate from one page to another.

Spider - A program that automatically fetches Web pages for search engines

URL - "Universal Resource Locator," this is the address of a web page

Web hosting – a hosting company that provides the server that your site will sit on

Important Marketing Distinctions

Marketing versus advertising: Advertising is only one function of marketing although it is often the most visible. One can usually live without advertising; one cannot live without marketing.

Marketing versus promotion: Promotion is a part of marketing. You can be a successful marketer without being a promoter.

Marketing versus sales: Marketing is not selling, although selling is a part of marketing.

REFERENCES

BANGS JR, DAVID H, *The Marketing Plans,* Dearborn Trade Publishing, 1995, 1998, 2002.

BLY, ROBERT W, *Fool-Proof Marketing,* John Wiley & Sons, Inc., 2003.

CRANDALL, RICK (ED*), Marketing Your Services: For People Who Hate to Sell,* McGraw-Hill, 2002.

JAMISON, MICHELLE, *Creating Your Client Information Package,* VA Self-Help Series, 2001.

JAMISON, MICHELLE, *Creating Your Marketing Materials,* VA Self-Help Series, 2001.

JAMISON, MICHELLE, *Website 101,* VA Self-Help Series, 2001.

LEVINSON, JAY CONRAD, *Mastering Guerrilla Marketing,* Houghton Mifflin Company, 1999.

Articles

OBRINGER, LEE ANN, *How Marketing Plans Work,* HowStuffWorks, Inc., 1998-2003.

LEDUC, BOB, *Target Marketing Strategy -- Find your own niche market,* 2000.